AUSTRALIA
The Wild Continent

AUSTRALIA
The Wild Continent

MICHAEL MORCOMBE

LANSDOWNE PRESS
Sydney·Auckland·London·New York

Captions from previous pages.

Page 4: The Northern Native-cat, denizen of tropical Australia, remains common, protected by the rugged wilderness of the country it inhabits. In the wild sandstone ranges of the Kimberleys and Arnhem Land this marsupial carnivore and other wildlife have secure refuge.

Page 5: One of Australia's most beautiful birds of prey, with white face, and bright cinnamon-brown, black-streaked underparts, the Square-tailed Kite is a rare species which is found in any habitat in Australia except the eastern coastal and south-eastern forested regions.

Page 6/7: A segment of wild southern coastline is preserved in the Fitzgerald River National Park. The unspoiled coastline has varied scenery and wildlife habitats, including river estuaries, ocean beaches and cliffs, sandplains with mallee and heaths, and granite ranges.

Captions for following pages

Page 10/11 Between the rounded domes of the Olgas, in central Australia, spinifex covers the stony ground. This needle-leaved grass is the dominant vegetation over a huge region of inland Australia, and is the preferred habitat of a great many birds, mammals and other wildlife.

Page 16/17: Raising its jagged hazy blue silhouette above lesser peaks of Tasmania's central highlands, Cradle Mountain dominates the alpine heathlands and forests. This landscape is a result of glaciation, when ice carved Cradle Mountain's jagged profile, and gouged from solid rock the basins of the alpine lakes.

Page 18: The red sand dunes of the central Australian deserts, like these at Ayers Rock, are among its most fascinating features. Upon their soft sand at daybreak can be found recorded the tracks of the nocturnal desert creatures; the patterns, shadows and colours make their curved and rippled contours visually rewarding as artistic subjects.

CONTENTS

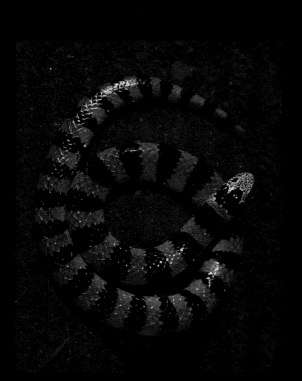

Page 19: Dense forests cover the lower slopes of Tasmania's south-western mountains. At Mount Field National Park, tall treeferns fill misty damp valleys. Waterfalls are fed from snowfields higher up the mountain.

Page 20/21: The Gilbert River, Queensland, like others of northern and inland Australia, is a refreshing scene in contrast to the surrounding dry sun-scorched landscape, with cool blues and greens of pools and river gums.

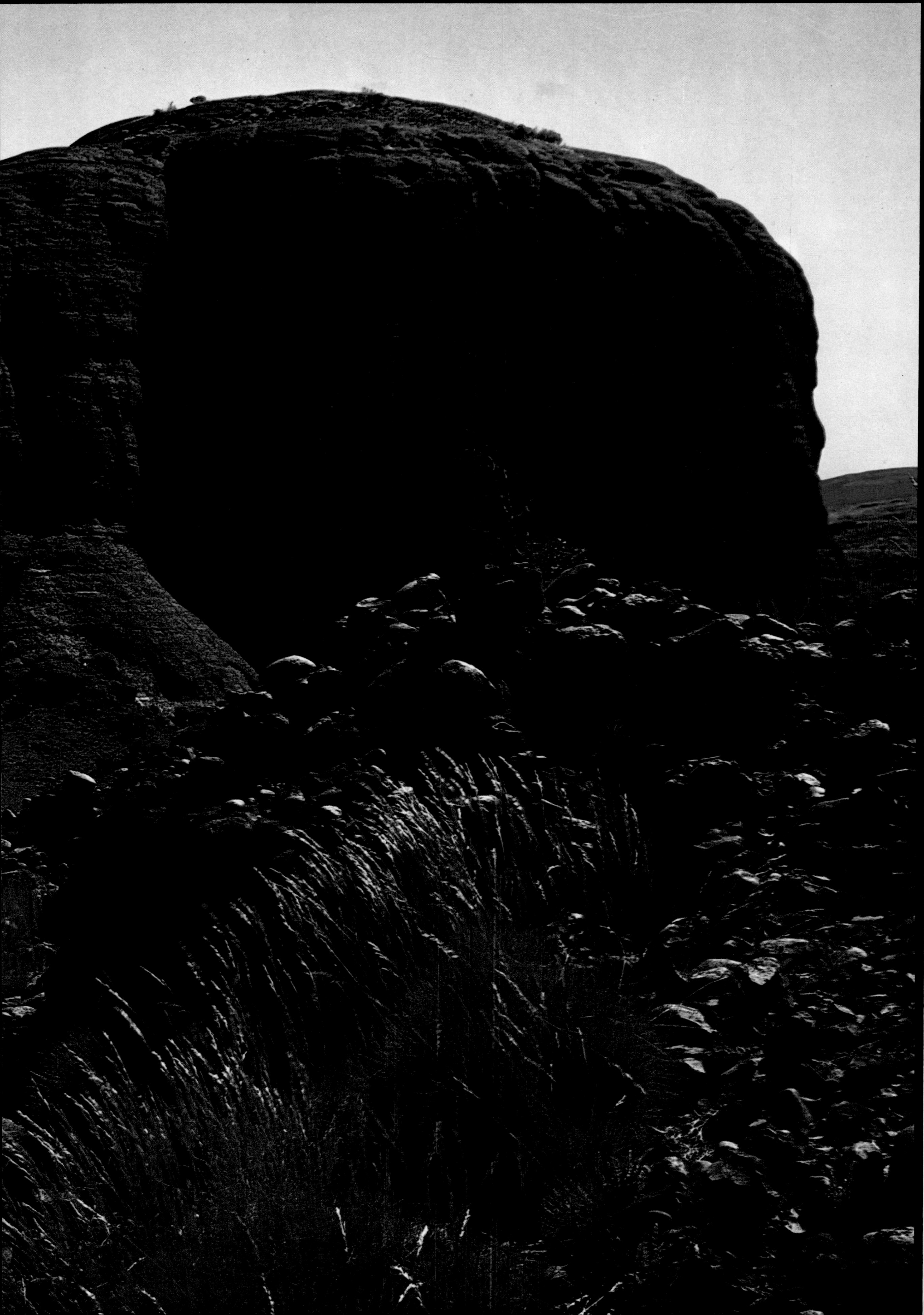

INTRODUCTION A CHANGING WILDERNESS

Wilderness can still be found on the Australian continent. Here landscapes unchanged by man owe their every detail to the forces of nature acting over the ages. Thousands of kilometres of the coastline remain which would show no sign of change, could their cliffs and beaches now be seen by pioneer navigators who first sighted them 370 years ago. There are still extensive tracts of country in the Kimberleys, in Arnhem Land, the western deserts, and south-western Tasmania, where there are no roads or tracks, and where there has probably never been the imprint of wheels upon their soils.

Australia has been isolated from the mainstream of world plant and animal evolution for such a length of time that much of its flora and fauna is unique. Even with the first arrival of man, there was insignificant change to Australia as a wild continent. As hunters and gatherers, the Aboriginal people lived in harmony with their environment. They saw their role as a part of the land, together with its creatures, rather than trying to re-shape their surroundings. By contrast, mankind in many other parts of the world has for thousands of years modified his environment by grazing his flocks, and clearing for crops, for villages and cities.

Due in part to the late beginning of habitation by European man, many parts of the continent remain rich and varied wilderness areas.

An equal if not greater force in the retention of wilderness values has been the forbidding nature of much of the Australian continent. The greater part of the population is crowded into urban areas situated in the climatically pleasant south-eastern and south-western corners of the continent. Remote from these centres of population, most of the large tracts of remaining natural environment are situated in far northern, western or central Australian regions.

But even close to the major cities remnants of natural environment survive, usually in places that were too rugged, or of too poor a soil, to find early use in agriculture. Many now have protection as national parks, fauna reserves, or as water catchment areas, in forestry use. This does not mean that all remaining wild landscapes or creatures of Australia are safe. Far from it, for there are constant pressures upon natural regions, which are all too often seen as wasted lands, that could be put to better and more profitable use for mining, agricultural, pastoral or other use generally destructive of the natural beauty, flora and fauna.

While interest in preservation of the original face and character of Australia has grown tremendously over the last decade, so has competition for land.

Among the wild regions remaining, is great diversity of scenery, from rainforests to deserts and mountain ranges. The scenic contrasts between these is striking, each holds its own plants and animals, each is a whole new world.

Rainforests are dominated by huge trees that compete for all the life-giving light that is available; their limbs interlock in all directions until a dense canopy of foliage is drawn over almost every opening. In this upper level is a world of sunlit greenery, with aerial gardens of huge Staghorn, Elkhorn and Birds Nest ferns, golden-flowered epiphytic orchids, brightly coloured butterflies, and superbly plumaged birds are rarely seen near the ground.

Below, at the rainforest floor, it can be so gloomy that only a few plants grow. The sunlight through the foliage is filtered to a perpetually gloomy greenish twilight. This is a world of dampness, in the summer wet season almost constant rain, dripping leaves, sodden ground, moist decaying logs with mosses, lichens and fungi.

In total contrast is Australia's arid interior. At that same time of year the mid-day heat becomes stifling, there is little or no shade, the glare of the intense sunlight hurts the eyes. Heated air rises with a spiralling twist, lifting a column of dust. The shimmering air above this sun-baked land distorts reality; mirages put reflecting pools of water into dry saltlakes, where hills and scrub appear mirrored with tantalizing reality. The gibber-stones of the plains polished by wind-blown sand, gleam and shimmer, every stone a tiny mirror bouncing back the glare of the sun. On the mulga scrub plains the dead and the scarcely living trees, their bare wood bleached, form a stark white contrast against red earth.

Although not a mountainous continent, Australia has some regions of impressive mountain scenery. Here are forests of tall gums with luxuriant undergrowth of treeferns, and fascinating mossy cool rainforests totally different in character from those of the tropics.

Most ruggedly spectacular are the mountain regions of Tasmania. Here is scenery of true alpine character, glaciated landforms, ice-carved cliffs, crystal-clear lakes and streams, jagged horizons and peaks.

Australia has through ages past been a lonely continent. The theory of continental drift reveals just how isolated from the rest of the world this continent has been. Originating as part of a much larger land mass some forty million years ago, it drifted free, separating from other slabs of the earth's crusts that were to be known as South America and Antarctica. Although Australia has drifted alone for more than thirty million years, it still shares from that common beginning, plants that are closely related to those of South America, and occur as fossils in Antarctica; the Antarctic Beech of Australian cool temperate rainforests is one example.

Above: The Eastern Grey Kangaroo *(Macropus giganteus)* is one of the largest of the kangaroos, over 180 cm tall. It inhabits forests and woodlands of eastern Australia, from northern Queensland to Victoria and Tasmania.

Opposite page: Islands around the Australian coastline are a last refuge for many small animals which, on the mainland, have been almost reduced to extinction since the arrival of European man. Bernier and Dorre Islands, in Shark Bay, north-western Australia, are sanctuaries for the Barred Bandicoot, now very rare in its former haunts elsewhere in Australia.

Also found in both Australia and South America are marsupials. Those of South America were almost eliminated in competition with other kinds of mammals, but the marsupials of Australia were isolated, secure from competition on their drifting piece of the earth's crust. Not until this slab or plate carrying Australia and New Guinea, moving northwards, came close to the islands of south-east Asia did the animals of Asia begin to reach this land. By the time the first men, the Aborigines, arrived, many placental mammals had become established — the bats and flying foxes, the native mice and rats. But on the whole, marsupials remained dominant up to the time of arrival of European man. In the comparatively short time since then, the balance has been tilted away from the ancient marsupial inhabitants, with the introduction and breeding of vast numbers of placental mammals, sheep, cattle, horses, cats, foxes and camels. Whether wild or domesticated, these have greatly changed the face of the continent.

The underlying landforms of Australia and their soils, together with climate, have shaped the plants to create for each region, a distinctive vegetation not duplicated elsewhere on earth.

This uniquely Australian vegetation in turn supports an animal population ranging from the smallest microbes and insects, through the whole spectrum of reptiles, birds and mammals. Each natural habitat, whether of rainforests, deserts or coasts, is a complete and self-sustaining, unique, natural ecosystem.

The divisions within this book are based on the different forms of Australian vegetation. The importance of the vegetation is that the plants directly exploit the basic potentials of soil and climate. These plants in turn are both habitat and food source for the animal life. The nature of the vegetation determines the composition of the wildlife of each region, the richness or paucity of species and numbers, whether these be endemic species, or whether the habitat shelters relic species.

The wild creatures of this continent are inseparably bound to the habitats for which they evolved; every animal has its preferred habitat. Some may not be able to survive in any other place, others are extremely adaptable, and occur in widely differing regions. In this book, the birds, reptiles and mammals have been placed in habitats, i.e. chapters, for which they seem most

appropriate. In the case of some wide-ranging species, these occur in the habitat in which they were photographed.

This is also a wild continent in the sense that it has a wealth of wildlife. Most conspicuous are the birds, attracting attention with calls and bright colours. Australia has about 775 species of birds, of which 600 breed on this continent or on nearby islands, and 125 are non-breeding visitors mostly from the northern hemisphere. There are also about 20 species that have been introduced since the beginning of European settlement.

Among these are some of the world's most distinctive birds. Some 360 species are found only on this continent, an indication that many are quite unlike those of other lands. Here are parrots and cockatoos displaying brilliant colours in the treetops, bowerbirds attending courtship arenas, honeyeaters in great numbers probing the flowers, and huge flightless birds.

Among the furred animals some are well known, the koala, the many kinds of kangaroo. But there is a host of others less well known; most are shy secretive creatures of the night. There are tiny but fierce marsupial-mice, gliders, ring-tailed and brush-tailed possums, potoroos, pademelons, bettongs, rat-kangaroos and kangaroo-rats.

Almost 400 species of reptiles inhabit the Australian continent. In the arid regions they are one of the most common forms of animal life.

Geckos may be found of a great variety of shapes and sizes; there are more than 40 Australian species. The Australian lizards include the skinks, with more than 100 species, and the dragons, which are small but in some cases quite dragon-like in appearance. The most startling of these is the Thorny Devil, which has an armour of sharp thick spines over head and body. Another spectacular dragon is the Frilled Lizard, which can suddenly erect an umbrella-like brightly coloured frill around its neck.

Found only in Australia is a group of burrowing lizards which are entirely legless and often very snake-like. These live underground, beneath rocks, forest debris or in dense vegetation where the snake-like wriggling of the body gives better propulsion than small legs. This deterioration of the legs, like flightlessness in birds, has become an advantage within certain habitats; with any major change in the

environment such specialization can become an impediment, and lead to extinction.

The most impressive of Australian reptiles are the monitors, or goannas. Although also found outside Australia, on this continent they have evolved into their greatest variety. Giants ten metres long which in the past roamed the inland plains have been extinct some three million years. But the Perentie remains, an awe-inspiring reptile at close quarters. This big monitor attacks its prey with speed and agility, sometimes employing its powerful and heavy tail to knock down and stun a victim.

Above: The shrub *Grevillea wickhamii* is common in the Northern Territory and northern parts of Western Australia, particularly in hilly rocky regions. Usually it flowers between May and October.

Opposite page: As this Brown Honeyeater *(Lichmera indistincta)* thrusts its curved bill into the tubular kangaroo-paw flower, in order to reach the nectar, it must bring the crown of its head up against the overhanging pollen-laden anthers.

HEATHLANDS AND SANDPLAINS

Heathlands and sandplains are Australia's wildflower country. More than any other habitat, it is the heaths, growing on the poorest sandy soils of both western and eastern sides of the continent, that support a tremendous diversity of flowering plants. These in turn attract a great variety and number of honeyeaters. When the heathlands are in full flower the bushland is alive with birds dashing from flower to flower, pausing for but an instant to probe for nectar with long curved bills. Their brisk activity, colours and song bring life to the bush. The heathlands and sandplains on a warm spring day can be as alive, with visible, audible activity, as any other Australian habitat. Under the warm sun of a calm spring day the hum of insects is a background to the spirited calls of the birds.

While many species — the larger, stronger flowers — are bird-pollinated, far more seek the attention of insects to transport their pollen. And the activity does not cease at nightfall. Some marsupials have become nectar specialists, and raid the heathland flowers under concealment of darkness.

Heaths are of many kinds, but all are shrub communities less than two metres, usually less than one metre high. This shrubbery is composed of a great many species, most of which are hard-leaved (sclerophyllous) and xeromorphic (woody), and there are few soft grasses or herbs. Heaths are principally a feature of the southern and eastern parts of Australia.

In the south they are on poor coastal sandplains and sandstone country, generally between ocean and forests; in tropical and sub-tropical regions the heaths are confined to areas of acidic soils in wet coastal districts. There are also small areas of dry mallee heaths, and alpine heathlands.

Although the rainfall received by most coastal heathlands is quite high, the amount available to the plants is usually much less as the water quickly disappears into the deep sand. Certain plant families tend to be dominant, the Proteaceae (*Banksia, Grevillea, Hakea, Lambertia*), the Myrtaceae (*Eucalyptus, Leptospermum, Melaleuca, Darwinia, Callistemon*), the Epacridae (*Gompholobium, Pultenaea, Kennedia*) and an abundance of Acacia species.

The species which make up the heathland communities are well adapted to the stresses of this habitat, particularly the low level of nutrition

available from the poor sands, and the greater frequency of fires which heathland areas appear to experience. There are many adaptations to these conditions, such as the usually small and hard-textured leaves, and extensive root systems. The roots include both surface networks for humus-layer nutrients, and deep taproots to reach water.

Heathlands support abundant animal populations. As well as the many birds, the mammals include the Western Grey Kangaroo, Red-necked Wallaby, Black-tailed Wallaby, Southern Potoroo, South-west Pigmy Possum, and Honey Possum. Among birds closely tied to heathland habitats are the Southern Emu-wren, Rufous Bristlebird, Chestnut-rumped Heath-wren, and Orange-bellied Parrot.

The floristically outstanding heathlands tend to occur on the opposite sides of the continent, down the east coast, and the south-western corner.

In south-eastern Queensland, a coastal strip known as the 'Wallum', north of Noosa and around Cooloola, and on Fraser Island, has low heath scrub with scattered banksia and eucalypt trees. A typical bird list can be compiled of this rich wildflower country: the Blue-faced Honeyeater, Scarlet Honeyeater, New Holland Honeyeater, White-cheeked Honeyeater, Southern Emu-wren, and various species of lorikeet.

On the opposite side of the continent, the heaths of Western Australia carry a large share of that State's famed wildflowers. Major heath areas are on the west coastal plains extending north from Perth almost to Shark Bay, and along the south coast as far east as Cape Arid.

Outstanding localities are at Kalbarri National Park, Nambung National Park, the Albany coastline, Cape Le Grand and Cape Arid National Parks. There are also many patches of heath on inland sandplains, while the heaths and low scrubs of the Stirling Ranges National Park contain exceptional and unique wildflowers.

In New South Wales, coastal heaths are a feature of the Myall Lakes National Park and Port Stephens on the northern coast, and of sandstone country around Sydney where the heaths are interspersed with dry eucalypt forest.

On the south coast, heaths are a major part of Ben Boyd National Park and the Nadgee Nature Reserve. Here the heaths are dominated by small shrubs such as grevilleas, boronias,

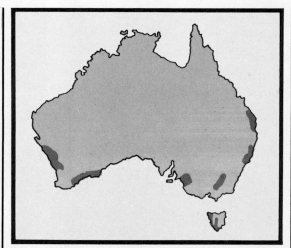

wax flowers, and the common heath, *Epacris impressa*. The low shrubbery gives shelter and protection for birds, the flowers attracting honeyeaters, such as the Tawny-crowned Honeyeater. The Barren Grounds Faunal Reserve, a heath area of the Illawarra Escarpment, has areas of sedge plants, with seed heads that make this an important habitat for the Swamp Parrot, *Pezoporus wallicus*.

Victoria has heathlands around Western Point on Wilson's Promontory, the Lakes National and Mallacoota National Parks, and the Mt. Richmond National Park near Portland. The coastal heaths extend into South Australia and occur behind the dunes and marshes of the Coorong.

Tasmania has coastal heaths in narrow strips down its eastern coast, as exemplified at Freycinet Peninsula National Park, and in north-western Tasmania at Rocky Cape National Park and Woolnorth.

Alpine heaths are an important segment of the highlands of south-eastern Australia, occurring on poor soils derived from granite and sandstone. These are located at Girraween and other National Parks in the granite belt of southern Queensland and northern New South Wales, the Hawkesbury and Blue Mountains sandstone country, the Grampians of Victoria, and Tasmanian areas of alpine heathlands.

Opposite page: Where strong winds from the sea have stripped vegetation and sand, tall spires of limestone remain; nearby, others exposed centuries ago rise above heathland vegetation and stabilized the sand. In the Nambung National Park, large areas of coastal heathland vegetation are preserved.

Left: The Honey Possum, a mouse-sized marsupial, is so dependent upon nectar as food that it has gradually evolved a long slender beak-like snout, with a tiny mouth at the tip, and a brush-tipped tongue rather like that of the nectar-eating birds. Its teeth are so small that they are quite insignificant, not being needed by an animal feeding upon nectar. So unusual is the Honey Possum, and apparently without any close relatives in the animal world, that zoologists have placed the Tarsipedidae in a family of its own. Confined to Australia's extreme south-western corner, the Honey Possum *(Tarsipes spencerae)* is found mostly in sandplain and sand heath country, which is abundant with large-flowered native plants such as banksias, dryandras and bottlebrushes. Although a skilful climber, the Honey Possum appears to spend a considerable time on the ground, where it is quite fast-moving. It is said to build a nest in dense foliage, but may take over an abandoned nest of a bird.

Above: On the sandplains of south-western Australia, the orange-flowered Christmas Tree *(Nuytsia floribunda)* comes into flower in mid-summer, each tree a blaze of colour visible at a great distance. No ordinary tree, this is one of the mistletoe family, and attaches itself to the roots of surrounding trees and shrubs, drawing nourishment from them, as do other mistletoes from the limbs of their host trees. On the windswept heathlands of the southern coast of Western Australia, this tree is often dwarfed in height; here it grows near Mississippi Point, in the Cape Le Grande National Park, at the western end of the Great Australian Bight. This tree appears to be insect-pollinated, and very fire resistant.

Right: Found in heathlands, semi-arid scrublands, and the undergrowth shrubbery of dry eucalypt forests, the Splendid Wren *(Malurus splendens)* has a wide distribution across Australia, from western parts of New South Wales, Queensland and Victoria, to Western Australia. In full sunlight, the male in breeding plumage is one of the most spectacular of all wrens, being, except for the black bands, a rich iridescent blue with silvery and purplish highlights. The eastern populations were formerly known as the Turquoise Wren and the Black-backed Wren. Like so many of the wrens, the Splendid Wren is usually seen in small family parties.

Left: The small insectivorous marsupial with the quaint common name of Dibbler is an extremely rare species. The name 'Dibbler' was used by Aborigines who assisted John Gilbert, pioneer collector of Australian zoological specimens, when they brought to him the first of these animals. Very few were ever collected, and none after 1884. By 1967, after 83 years, this species was assumed to be extinct. But in that year two were discovered by the author; shown above, one of these seeks nectar or small insects on a banksia flower. It is thought that the nectar is attractive to these and other mammals during warm dry summer months.

Right: Tasmanian heaths are in places of a sub-alpine character. Like those of other regions, these heaths are dominated by woody shrubs, of which the tea-trees are common. As with sandplain heathlands, the soil is poor. In alpine heath communities are many plants unique to Tasmania, including the Tea-tree *(Leptospermum rupestre)* and the Varnished Gum *(Eucalyptus vernicosa)*. *Richea scoparia,* with massed spikes of crimson, pink, yellow or white flowers, is a prominent alpine wildflower peculiar to Tasmania. Unusual features of alpine heaths are the cushion plants of the alpine plateaux, and the button-grass of the lowland plains.

Previous page: Although most sandplain regions are flat and rather low-lying, some of Australia's western coast plains which were once near sea level have been uplifted. The Murchison River, which meandered across the sandplains, was rejuvenated. The uplifting accelerated its flow and carved its river bed deeper, eventually cutting a long deep gorge into the colourful sandstone. The Kalbarri gorges twist and turn across the sandplains of what is now a low plateau. Across the sandplains the low heaths include stands of low *Verticordias,* while scattered small trees bear orange or yellow *Banksia* flower spikes, or long white *Grevillea* plumes.

Above: In mid-summer the sandplains of Australia's western coast turn brilliant golden in almost unbelievable massed display, where tall slender-stemmed plants, growing in close-packed profusion, together open out their umbrella-crowns of tiny feathery-edged flowers. These plants grow rapidly upwards, and reach almost full height of almost a metre, before branching out into a crown of small leaves and flowers. During second and subsequent years it adds several centimetres, just enough to form a new domed crown of foliage and golden flowers. Eventually some plants may reach a height of nearly 2 m, and support a 30 cm wide mass of golden flowers at the top of its pencil-thick stem.

Right: On the sandplains when the heaths are flowering there is an almost unceasing drift of tenuous bird-song, lilting bell-like notes, some nearby, others far away. Their background melody, coming across at times faint, then strong, clear and pleasant, slightly sad, is somehow in keeping with the windswept loneliness of the open plains. These Tawny-crowned Honeyeaters *(Phylidonyris melanops)* common birds of sandplains and heathlands, are more easily heard than seen. Tawny-crowns occur in south-eastern and south-western Australia. Their nest, hidden in a low bush, can be quite difficult to find. The birds rarely fly directly to it, but land some distance away, and sneak to the nest, keeping out of sight in the low dense vegetation.

Left: The tiny Emu-wrens are among Australia's most unusual small birds, but are not well known, for their secretive habits make them quite difficult to find. This species, the Southern Emu-wren, inhabits swampy dense low vegetation, and the heathlands of coastal dunes. Much of their time is spent on the ground, where they run mouse-like through the bushes. Most remarkable is their tail, of an open lacy filament structure that resembles the pattern of emu feathers, hence the name emu-wren. The transparent appearance of the tail distinguishes it immediately from other wrens, whose tails appear solid. The Southern Emu-wren *(Malachurus stipiturus)* is found in south-eastern and south-western Australia, and also in Tasmania.

Below and below right: Spinebill honeyeaters, the male much brighter in plumage colours than the female, probe for nectar in flowers which are adapted for pollination by birds. A unique partnership exists between plants and animals of the Australian bushland. Many birds, mammals and insects live upon the nectar and pollen of native flowering trees, shrubs and small plants. These plants in turn have evolved shapes and structures to make use of their animal visitors. There are great differences between flowers evolved for insect pollinators, and those adapted for birds.

Right: The Royal Hakea *(Hakea victoriae)* has been described as one of the most spectacular foliage plants in the world. The tall slender shrubs have very large leaves, so tough and rigid, spiny-edged, that they seem to have been cut from jagged sheet metal rather than belonging to living plants. But their striking colour more than compensates for their repelling texture. New leaves are at first bright green, soon turning bright yellow and with dark green areas yellow-veined. By the following year, these leaves have darkened to deep orange, and in the third year, deep red. Close-up, each leaf has an intricate network of veins in a lighter tone.

Right: On the coastal sand heathlands of Australia's south coast west of the Bight, between Israelite Bay and the Fitzgerald River, the Showy Banksia *(Banksia speciosa)* may be found flowering in any month of the year. Equally attractive as the large yellow flower heads, are the sawtooth pattern leaves, up to 40 cm in length. The coastal sandplains of the region have many species of banksia. Their colours vary from crimsons through yellows and orange tones to dull browns. In size they range from small trees to prostrate species which have underground stems and flowers and leaves that push up from the sand. It has been recorded that birds and mammals pollinate many of these Banksias, but it is interesting to speculate what creatures would be the pollinators of some of the species with flowers on the ground.

Above: The visual interest of some native plants is not only in their flowers, but also in foliage, bark or other feature. In the case of the sandplains shrub *Banksia baxteri,* the seeds which follow after the yellow flowers are rather fascinating. It seems that of all the hundreds of flowers that are packed around each of its large domed flower heads, only a few set seed. It is common to see the spike, the centre of the original flower mass, with just one or two of the reddish, furry-surfaced new seed capsules embedded, creating rather weird abstract shapes. After a time the colour is lost, but the hard seed capsules remain attached for years, until the tree is scorched by fire, or dies, when the seeds will be released.

SWAMPS, LAKES AND RIVERS

Australia has relatively few wetlands, a consequence of the low rainfall of most parts. In the arid central regions, rivers seldom flow. But occasionally, as after tropical cyclones, floods cover vast areas creating temporary wetlands of great extent. Tropical northern rivers flood annually, replenishing the extensive billabongs and swamps of their floodplains.

The wetlands of eastern coastal Australia are more permanent, and rich in bird and other life, but even in these most humid parts of the continent, wetlands are but a very small portion of the total environment. Many of the small swamps scattered around coastal south-eastern and south-western regions are dependent upon winter rains, and are dry in drought years. Inland, the Murray-Darling River system often floods to fill extensive billabongs which are breeding grounds of vast flocks of birds.

The wetlands of tropical northern Australia are a fascinating environment. Here occur the giant waterlilies of deep pink, and white. Birds are abundant, flocks of thousands may be seen of some species. Here may be seen tall stately Jabiru, Brolgas, and several species of egret. There are Royal and Yellow-billed Spoonbills, Glossy and White Ibis, Burdekin Duck, Green Pigmy Geese, Magpie Geese, and Whistle-ducks.

In the rivers and swamps are the small Freshwater Crocodiles, and in some inland rivers and lagoons, the large and dangerous Estuarine Crocodile. Smaller reptiles are more common, and include several species of water goannas, tortoises, and pythons with a preference for damp places. Among the curiosities is the Archerfish, which with accurately directed squirts of water shoots down insects and spiders.

Heavy rainfall of the tropical wet season floods huge areas, mostly on the coastal floodplains of the rivers of the Northern Territory and the Kimberley region of Western Australia. These swamps gradually dry out after the wet season, until only the deepest and most permanent pools remain. Wildlife, spread widely across almost the entire landscape in the wet season, becomes concentrated upon remaining wetlands, and more easily observed. There are also several man-made wetlands where access for observation of water birds may be more convenient. These include the Fogg Dam Bird Sanctuary, near Humpty Doo, south-east of Darwin.

In north-eastern Queensland, major wetlands occur at the southern end of Cape York Peninsula, to the west of Cooktown, on the Normanby, Laura and Kennedy River systems which drain into Princess Charlotte Bay. The Burdekin River Valley, west of Ingham, has an area known as the Valley of Lagoons, which is an outstanding wetlands region.

At Townsville, on the north-eastern coast of Queensland, one of Australia's most famous wetlands habitats offers the sight of great numbers of birds. The Town Common Fauna and Flora Reserve has in its 3200 hectares both saltmarsh lagoons and mangroves. On the Common have been recorded some 180 species of birds, 40 species of reptiles and 20 species of amphibians. The Townsville Common is, however, most famed for its huge flocks of Brolgas. Several thousand have been observed here during the winter dry season, when the drying out of smaller wetland areas concentrates Brolgas and other water birds in the direction of the Common.

On the northern New South Wales coast the Myall Lakes National Park has lakes surrounded by high sand dunes. In the damp hollows of the area grow paperbarks, swamp oaks, and crimson bottlebrushes. Red-necked Wallabies, Swamp Wallabies, Brown Antichinus, and the New Holland Mouse occur there.

Inland, in southern Queensland, important wetlands occur at Umbercollie Lagoon near Goondiwindi and Nangran Lagoon near Condamine. The Nangran Lagoon is said to be the most southerly location of the large pink Lotus Lily.

When the inland rivers of northern and central New South Wales run high, the water spreads across the countryside, forming lakes and marshes upon which water birds converge to form huge nesting colonies. One of the most famous of these is the Macquarie Marshes of central western New South Wales; another, on the Gwydir River, is a marsh known as the Watercourse. On these, the colonies of birds vary their nesting sites from year to year, depending upon which rivers are flowing.

North-eastern coastal New South Wales has wetlands along its coastal lowlands where rivers that rush down waterfalls and gorges of the New England escarpment, flood low-lying areas of coastal flats. Angourie National Park includes Lake Woolowyah and Lake Arragan, while

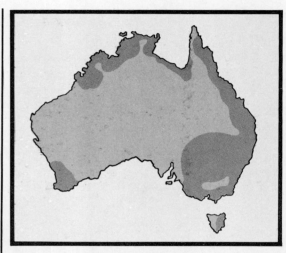

there are swamps in Red Rock National Park and Hat Head National Park near Kempsey. Paperbark swamps range along the Wooli River near Coffs Harbour.

In southern Australia, major wetlands occur in south-eastern coastal areas around the mouth of the Murray at the Coorong, and at Bool Lagoon and Big Heath near Naracoorte. Victoria has lakes and swamps along many parts of its coast. In Port Phillip Bay, there are marshes on Mud Island and at the mouth of the Werribee River. East of Wilson's Promontory, there are wetlands habitats of coastal lakes and swamps extending to Mallacoota Inlet.

The major inland wetlands of the south-east are found on the Murray River, where large swamps occur, such as at Burmah State Forest, Kow Swamp, and Hattah Lakes National Park. These swamps carry huge breeding colonies of spoonbills, egrets, Nankeen Night Herons, and several species of ibis.

Western Australia is mostly arid, and the major permanent wetlands are those of the south-west corner. Although one-third of the Swan Coastal Plain was wetlands, much has been filled in for agriculture or other purposes, and only a fraction now remains. Numerous wheatbelt lakes are breeding areas for water birds, but are dry in years of low rainfall.

Opposite page: In the tropical wet season the monsoonal rains flood vast areas of swamps along the Northern Territory coastal plains. Here the Alligator River, the South Alligator River, the Mary and the Adelaide Rivers pour their waters into swamps and across wide floodplains.

35

Right: Low over the reedbeds a Swamp Harrier circles, gliding on upcurved wings; its fast sweep carries it abruptly from screening reeds to open water. In an explosion of spray and beating wings the waterbird flocks scatter: grebes diving, ducks and swans beating across the surface into flight, herons, egrets and ibis lifting heavily yet gracefully into the air. Once aloft, each seeks others of its kind, and in the security of the tight formations of their flocks, circle and watch. The Harrier drops, almost touches the water with its talons, lifts up and ascends swiftly with powerful slow wingbeats. As it rises higher and further away, the water birds begin to splash down on the water again. But no sooner have the flocks settled and timid coots, swamp hens and grebes emerged from the reeds, than the Harrier is again in their midst, and the air once more is filled with a confusion of birds. It seems the Harrier is playing. It makes no effort to pursue, but seems rather to enjoy the pandemonium that its sudden appearance, as it skims in low through the treetops, causes among the feeding, preening and dozing assembly of birds.

When seriously hunting, the Swamp Harrier must be able to take its prey almost at will. As its young grow larger in the floating nest in the centre of the swamp reedbed, the Harrier begins to bring food just before dawn, and returns frequently at ten-minute intervals, with ducklings, young grebes, or rats. The feeds lengthen to half an hour, sometimes an hour, to mid-day, and there may be intervals of three or four hours between feeds during the afternoon.

Above: An extremely secretive inhabitant of the reedbeds, the Little Grass-bird *(Megalurus gramineus)* is more often heard than seen, its rather mournful soft calls being a common sound of swamps of south-eastern and south-western Australia. But the birds sneak through dense reedbeds and usually manage to keep vegetation between themselves and any observer. The nest, a solidly built structure of reeds and grass with a deep, warmly lined egg cavity, has often a curved feather of a swamp-hen or other large water bird, built into the rim and arching over to form a hood. These birds keep to the reedbeds most of the time. But they at times travel great distances, even across semi-desert country, to reach isolated inland swamps. The Little Grass-bird is one of a host of reedbed birds. The frantically busy, crowded life of the wetlands could be told through the life of any of its host of birds, mammals, reptiles or insects. But the fascinating world of the swampland habitat, which gives an initial impression of being an unpleasant muddy, murky place, is relatively unknown to most people. A swamp, or equally the reedbeds and waters of a lake, is a world apart, as different from the surrounding woodland, forest or scrub, as is a city from its rural surrounds.

Above: Shallow lakes form ideal wetlands habitat for water birds; this typical small lake is, for much of the year, shallow enough for long-legged wading birds to feed over much of its area. Around its margins, paperbark trees and reedbeds provide shelter and nest sites. Common on the open waters and margins of such lakes of southern Australia are Black Swans, Avocets, White-faced Herons and Stilts, in great numbers. There are ducks of many species, especially Mountain Duck, Grey Teal and Black Duck. Lakes such as this are fascinating places for bird watching, with the aid of binoculars. The number of species crowded on to its waters, around its shores, its reedbeds and surrounds is far greater than in almost any land area. Not only are there to be seen the resident Australian birds, but also, in summer, the many Asiatic wading birds that migrate to Australia to avoid the northern hemisphere winter.

One of the most graceful of the waders is the Red-necked Avocet, **above** (*Recurvirostra novaehollandiae*). This may be seen in most inland parts of eastern Australia, and most of Western Australia except the forested south-west corner. This bird does not occur in the tropical north, nor in some of the central Australian desert country. However, they will sometimes be seen

in quite arid country where heavy rain has filled the salt lakes and claypans. Avocets nest in colonies or small groups, the nests being slight hollows in the ground, usually built up with sticks. The site is generally a small island in a shallow claypan or lake, where there is some protection for these ground-nesting birds against predators. The young when hatched are fluffy little creatures, already with long pointed bills and long legs; as soon as all eggs have hatched the family leaves the nest for the safety of the water. The Red-necked Avocet is not found outside Australia.

The White Egret, **right,** also known as the Large Egret *(Egretta alba)* is found throughout Australia, and is likely to be seen wherever there is water — coastal estuaries, mangroves, or flooded pasture lands. It is most often seen at a distance, hunting, standing tall, upright, motionless, alert, or with head drawn back, spear-like bill ready to be driven downwards. It stares fixedly into the water, waiting, then suddenly the crooked neck, like a spring released, snaps straight, is driven down to impale a small fish, frog, or other prey. The nest is a platform of sticks, usually in a tree growing in a

swamp, and in a colony with many egrets and other water birds.

Right: A Plumed Egret wades through a Northern Territory paperbark swamp amid bright yellow water lily flowers. Australia has three species of graceful white egrets. This, the Plumed *(Egretta intermedia)* can be distinguished from the much larger White Egret in the breeding season by the filamentous plumes hanging down the breast as well as down the back. The White Egret has only the back plumes. Identification is complicated by the strange colour changes that occur. In the breeding season the normally yellow bill becomes red, and the yellowish-green bare facial skin turns blue-green. The nest is a platform of sticks in a tree, usually in a swamp, in company with many other nesting water birds in a large colony.

Left: Australia has Green and Gold Bell Frogs in both south-eastern and south-western regions. Although listed as separate species, some individuals of east and west are nearly identical. They can only be identified with the knowledge that if the frog came from southern districts of eastern Australia, it is the species *Litoria raniformis,* or from the south-west of the continent, it is the Western Green and Gold Bell Frog, *Litoria moorei.* Another almost identical species, of eastern New South Wales and Victoria, is the Green and Gold Bell Frog, *Litoria aurea.* These bell frogs are mostly aquatic, being usually seen in vegetation in or beside permanent water, such as swamp reedbeds or paperbark trees around lakes or lagoons.

Right: A brightly coloured small freshwater crayfish throws up its claws in a threatening display intended to keep its enemies at bay, then scuttles off to its burrow in a swamp or creek bank. This species is known as the Corchie *(Euastacus spinifer)* which inhabits south-eastern Queensland and north-eastern New South Wales, and grows to a length of 20 cm. Usually the colour is brownish or greenish-brown, with some red; specimens which have large areas of red can be quite spectacular. At certain times, perhaps caused by rainfall or water level changes, these freshwater crayfish leave their burrows and wander. They will most often be seen on wet nights.

Previous page: The shallow margins of a small lake glow golden. The early morning sunlight has illuminated golden-green algae growth revealed by falling water levels. This lake, filled by heavy rain in the catchment rivers, at this time of year was a haven for large flocks of water birds, especially of Mountain Ducks and Black Swans. At other times, this same swamp is dry. These small samphire bushes, which here are draped with golden algae water weed, are then dark green. Where large rafts of waterfowl float, there are usually small land birds, Splendid Wrens and White-fronted Chats, flying low among the bushes. Earlier in the year, the Mountain Duck were dispersed widely across the countryside as pairs selected their nest hollows and hatched out their young. Later, they arrived with their young on these larger lakes, congregating in large numbers.

Right: The Black Swan (*Cygnus atratus)* is one of the most famed of Australian birds. At times to be seen in almost any part of Australia, including deserts on the rare occasions that very heavy rains fill claypan lakes, the Black Swan also visits fresh, brackish or estuarine waters. The nest, almost a miniature island of reeds and water weeds, is around a metre in diameter. It floats usually in dense reeds or other swamp vegetation, but sometimes on open shallow lakes. In southern Australia, nesting occurs during winter, between May and September, when water levels are high in the swamps. In the north nesting is later in the summer wet season. The Black Swan was an early discovery, being recorded by the Dutch navigator Vlaming in 1697, when he was exploring the Swan River, now the site of Perth.

Left: Within Australia it has become a custom to refer to the members of one family of turtles as 'tortoises', and this is very useful in distinguishing them from the larger marine turtles. Although the members of this group are quite distinctive in having webbed and jointed hands and feet rather than paddle-shaped limbs, and a long neck that is folded sideways when the head is pulled under the shell, rather than retracted by vertical folding, they are nevertheless called 'turtles' elsewhere in the world. Tortoises are denizens of swamps, lakes and rivers and are widely distributed in eastern and northern Australia. This particular species, *Emydura Australis,* is an inhabitant of the Kimberley region.

Right: One of the most common and familiar of the birds of the wetlands, roadside ditches and wet pastures is the White-faced Heron *(Ardea novaehollandiae)*. It is found throughout Australia, including on occasions the arid central regions. On the shallow lake margins it is often in company with stilts, long-legged black and white birds, of which there are two species. The Pied or Black-winged Stilt *(Himantopus himantopus)* occurs throughout Australia except for a few of the most heavily forested and mountainous regions, and the most arid of central Australian deserts. More rare is the Banded Stilt *(Cladorhynchus leucocephalus)* which is found in western Victoria, eastern parts of South Australia north to the vicinity of Lake Eyre, and also in south-western Australia. This Stilt chooses remote places for nesting in huge colonies of up to twenty thousand nests, on islands of large shallow inland lakes, when filled by heavy rain.

Above: Lily lagoons are a feature of the river floodplains of northern Australia, and each seems to be dominated by one or the other of two species of large waterlily. The Giant Waterlily *(Nymphaea gigantea)* has very large round leaves which float flat on the water, and flowers of white, pink, magenta or blue held well above the leaves and the water. The other, the Lotus Lily *(Nelumbo nucifera)* is distinctively different, having leaves not floating flat but held more or less vertically and usually well above the water, as high or higher than the deep pink flowers. The northern lagoons are the home of many birds and other wetland wildlife. Some are very specialised for this habitat. The Jacana or Lotus Bird has long fine toes that spread right across the floating waterlily leaves, enabling it to walk easily across the swamps. As the countryside dries out at the end of the wet season, the water birds become concentrated in great variety on the more permanent swamps and lagoons. Green Pygmy-geese are often to be seen in small parties among the blue and pink waterlilies of the lagoons. Other birds are the Pied Goose, and the Water Whistle-duck.

Above: In the reflections in the quiet dark waters of a river pool is summarised much of the character of Australia's tropical north. On the surface of the water float water lily leaves, and reflected between these are the typically tropical Australian shapes of the pandanus palms which fringe almost every watercourse of northern Australia. At the rocky source of this creek were trees of the bright orange-flowered Darwin Woollybutt, and tall shrubs of *Grevillea pteridifolia,* also orange-flowered. But once the stream reached the flat grassy woodland plains its banks supported pink-flowered Swamp Bloodwood trees.

In just 1 or 2 km of the creek's course a remarkable variety of wildlife was seen. Among the green pandanus Crimson Finches make a colourful sight with their crimson and black plumage. The rank grasses along tropical watercourses are the habitat of two species of wrens, of the 'fairy-wren' group. One is the Red-backed Wren, the males black with crimson back; the second is the Purple-crowned Wren, a most unusual species whose only bright colour is the lilac or purple of the top of its head.

Above such pools as this, hanging from drooping foliage out over the water, the large pendant nests of Bar-breasted Honeyeaters are quite common. Below, skimming over the water, a fast-flying Azure Kingfisher or Little Kingfisher may be glimpsed for an instant.

The moist poolside vegetation and rocks are the territory of many kinds of frogs. Tortoises, water pythons and water monitors may be seen in or near the water. In large-leaved trees, especially along the waterside, the leaf nests of the Green Tree Ants are worth both observing and avoiding.

Left: Australia has many species of monitors, which include some of the largest of all lizards; in Australia these are usually called 'goannas'. Five species have adopted an aquatic life, and feed largely upon small fish and frogs, some living in marine and mangrove habitats, others preferring rivers and lagoons. This, Mertens Water Monitor *(Varanus mertensi)* occurs in far northern Australia, and was photographed at Jim Jim Falls, western Arnhem Land. In a large pool at the foot of the falls it was seen to have a consistent pattern of behaviour, slipping into the water to hunt fish for ten minutes, then basking for up to half an hour on a boulder.

Right: Floating water weed makes a lawn-like surface across swamp water beneath paperbark trees. This scene is typical of countless numbers of swamps and lake edges around coastal parts of Australia. Paperbark trees are characteristic of wet areas, occurring in swamps of the tropical north, as well as eastern and southern coastal regions. Paperbark trees are a most important habitat for shelter and for nesting. Thick-trunked old paperbarks provide hollows, especially where burnt during dry seasons. In these, or in cavities formed at the junction of thick limbs, nest such birds as the Black Bittern, Black Duck, Chestnut Teal, Grey Teal, Pink-eared Duck and Wood Duck. If the swamp is a colonial nesting site, higher in the paperbarks are hundreds of stick nests built by herons, egrets, night-herons, and cormorants. In the outer foliage will be the nesting sites of smaller birds, often where the foliage droops down over the water.

Right: The golden-green algae, a form of water weed, resembles translucent sheets of golden spider webs. Algae is left spread over small shrubs as the water level of a lake falls below its abnormally high flood level.

Right: The Nankeen Night-heron is found throughout Australia. Unusually, it hunts at night, patrolling shallow swamps, river edges, lake shores, stabbing with long pointed bill at fish, frogs and crustaceans. During the day it roosts in dense foliage of trees, usually those bordering swamps or lakes. The Nankeen Night-herons *(Nycticorax caledonicus)* nest in colonies, usually in company with egrets, herons and cormorants, and often take the opportunity to take from unattended nests, eggs or small chicks. During the breeding season three long white plumes project from the black cap of the head. In tropical northern Australia these herons, along with most other water birds, nest during the summer wet season, and in southern Australia, during the spring months. The population of Night-herons is linked with rainfall and abundance of aquatic food; at times there have been 'explosions' of numbers, under favourable conditions. This can be boosted still further under such circumstances by the breeding of birds still in immature plumage, of brownish, grey and white striped upper parts, and white-spotted wings.

Left: Around Australia's coastline, wherever there are sandy beaches interspersed with rocky coasts, and especially where there are sandplains or sand heathlands along the coast, the wind-blown sand of dunes can isolate small rivers from the sea. Lakes are formed behind dunes, and usually rivers or creeks flow into these lakes, and seep through the sand barrier to the sea. Some of the best known of such coastal lakes are found on Queensland's Fraser Island. But similar lakes and swamps occur in many other parts of the Australian coast, as at Western Port, and the Gippsland Lakes of Victoria, and the Coorong of South Australia. Shown here is a lake near the ocean at Two People's Bay, on the south coast of Western Australia.

Right: Ants climb the tiny ladders of stiff white hairs to reach the slippery brink of the insectivorous pitcher plant *(Cephalotis follicularis)*. Any small creature that ventures over the rim is likely to fall into the pool of digestive liquid at the bottom, and is unlikely to escape. The pitchers are highly modified leaves, which by digesting insects, supplement the plant's food supply. This plant grows around the waterlogged margins of swamps, where the soil nutrients, especially nitrogen, are deficient.

SPINIFEX AND OTHER ARID GRASSLANDS

Against the black-shadowed depths, bright green specks speed together in tight formation, so far down in the hundred-metre depths of the gorge that they could pass unnoticed but for their calls echoing upwards. Each flock, of five to thirty birds, would sweep into sight around the far bend, keeping perhaps twenty metres above the river pools. In less than a minute, they vanish from sight behind cliffs far along the gorge. Before they have gone another flock is usually on its way through, following the same course.

These birds were Budgerigars, apparently crossing the range by following the long gorge. There must have been several small flocks each minute; for how long, how many hours or days the migration continued, is unknown, but the total number of birds must have been tremendous.

This spectacle can be seen at Red Gorge in the Hamersley Ranges, where a lookout is situated on the rim of the gorge at a point where two narrower but equally deep canyons meet. The view into the great chasms is awe-inspiring, probably for sheer vertical depths, unequalled in any other part of Australia.

Above the gorges, the plateau-like range top is clothed in spinifex. This semi-arid landscape is usually a colour pattern of gold against dark brown rock, until the touch of rain might bring a change to green or brown.

Occasionally, budgerigars may be seen in huge flocks across the vast spinifex grasslands of north-western and central Australia. These birds were all headed in the same direction, presumably to a more auspicious region. In crossing the Hamersleys, the highest ranges in the western half of the continent, they may have found the route through the gorge easiest. Perhaps it was the most exciting — the sheer exhilaration of dashing at speed between close rock walls with river pools close below, the sky a narrow strip far above.

Spinifex is the dominant vegetation of more than twenty per cent of the Australian continent, principally in central and north-western Australia. In those regions it forms a hummocky cover across clay plains, sand dunes and rocky ranges; it is usually the dominant vegetation. But in addition there are many regions where spinifex is a ground cover beneath mulga, mallee or woodland.

Spinifex is technically known as arid hummock grassland. There are about twenty species belonging to two genera, *Triodia* and *Plectrachne*. Every species has its own preferred region and type of habitat. One species may be found on rocky hills of Central Australia, another on similar hills of north-western Australia, and others again on red sand dunes, on sandstone country, or stony creekbeds.

Most species of spinifex are extremely unpleasant to encounter. Each plant branches repeatedly to form many interlocking stems, all with long stiff needle-tipped leaves pointing outwards, building a low rounded hummock of the shape and deadly effect of a Spiny Anteater. With most spinifexes, it is not possible to insert a hand, even slowly, gently, into the spiny mass, unless wearing gloves.

The hummocks are usually about a half-metre maximum height, but can spread to form a circle up to ten metres diameter. Tall flower and seed stalks sent up in the months after rain may reach a metre and more in height, and *en masse* have the appearance of a field of ripening wheat.

These almost impenetrable fortresses shelter a number of animals. Some, such as the Rufous-crowned Emu-wren and Spinifex Bird, live exclusively in spinifex. So well adapted to this environment is the Rufous-crowned Emu-wren that even when a party of these tiny birds is within several metres distance, and calling, they can be difficult to see. Sometimes there is a momentary glimpse, which lasts too briefly to bring binoculars to bear upon the bird, as it scurries mouse-like from one clump to another. Often the presence of these birds goes completely un-noticed and unsuspected, until their calls attract attention. But so high-pitched are these calls, so like the faint high scratchy calls of grasshopper or cicadas of the spinifex, that the calls cannot be heard by some people, and are, if heard, often ignored as being insect sounds. The Rufous-crowned Emu-wren is similar to the Southern Emu-wren, but shorter-tailed, and bright rufous-brown on the crown of the head. Its nest is securely built into the spinifex hummock, as is that of the boldly coloured Painted Firetail Finch.

A great many reptiles live in spinifex; when they dash for cover in these deadly refuges they are very hard to find and capture. The Aborigines used fire in their pursuit, burning one hummock after another, capturing the goannas, skinks, snakes and geckos forced out by the heat.

Another type of arid grassland is

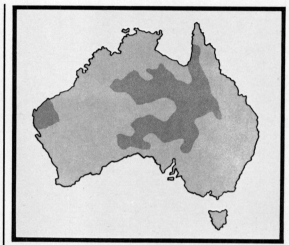

that which occurs in western Queensland and the Northern Territory. This is the arid tussock grassland, which is dominated by Mitchell Grass (Astraleba) which is softer, and forms tussocks rather than rounded hummocks.

Spinifex can be seen in the national parks of most States, usually as ground cover beneath mallee or mulga. Landscapes where spinifex is the dominant vegetation of ranges can be seen in the Northern Territory at Ormiston Gorge and other national parks of the MacDonnell Ranges, and at Mt Olga. In north-western Australia, at the Chichester, Rudall River and Hamersley Ranges National Parks, are vast areas of spinifex-covered ranges. Spinifex on sand country is a feature of north-western Australia, and can be seen to extend with apparent endlessness, along Highway One, between Carnarvon and Broome.

Opposite page: This waterfall, set in arid spinifex-clad ranges of north-western Australia on occasions thunders down the full width of its gorge. But from flood levels it quickly subsides, until a steady trickle is reached, almost permanently fed by springs deep beneath the ranges.

Above: Today this carnivorous marsupial is known as the Mulgara, a name given by the Aborigines of the desert regions it inhabits. It has also the name, Cannings Little Dog, having been seen on Canning's pioneering treks to establish a stock route across the Great Sandy Desert. The Mulgara *(Dasycercus cristicauda)* inhabits spinifex grasslands, stony and sand dune desert country, from south-western Queensland to the Pilbara region of north-western Australia. Not surprisingly in largely treeless regions, it is a terrestrial hunter, which will overpower other small mammals, ground birds and small reptiles. Scientific studies of Mulgara have shown that it is able to survive in the most arid and hot deserts without ever drinking water. Its body chemistry is such that it is able to obtain sufficient water from the bodies of its prey. At the same time its water loss, especially of urine, has been greatly reduced. Being a nocturnal hunter, it avoids the greatest heat of the day by remaining in its deep, cool, more humid burrows.

Right: Patterns of shadows cast by spinifex, blend with the camouflage patterns of a Bustard chick. Unable to fly, the chick squats and remains frozen at the first sign of danger, and is difficult to find. At the same time the parents feign injury, fluttering noisily on the ground as if unable to fly, while gradually drawing the intruder away from the hiding place of the chick. Commonly known as the 'bush turkey', the Bustard *(Ardeotis australis)* is a solidly built bird that stands about one metre tall. The adult birds have a haughty upright posture, and pace across the grassland plains and savannah woodlands with slow deliberate steps, unhurried, curious: In their overall grey-brown patterned plumage the adult Bustards blend effectively with the prevailing colours of dry spinifex or grass. There is a black head-cap, and white feathers hang, lace-like, down the breast. Bustards nest on the ground, one or sometimes two eggs being laid. Like the young, these are camouflage-patterned, in olive-brown with darker brown streaks and blotches.

The finch family contains many small and usually colourful seed-eating birds, distinguished by their short powerful bill. Some, like the Gouldian Finch, Painted and Red-eared Firetails, are among the most colourful of small Australian birds, with boldly patterned plumage. The majority of species inhabit northern grasslands and savannah woodlands, but a few occur in dense southern forests. For most of the year some finches form large and conspicuous flocks, which break up as the birds pair and select nest territories. Of the total of 115 species in the finch family, 19 occur in Australia, and 14 of these are found only in Australia. This family of finches *(Estrildidae)* are found in Asia, Africa and Australia and contains also the waxbills, mannikins and Java sparrows which are not found in Australia. Finches of another family *(Fringillidae)* occur in Europe, America and elsewhere, and include the grosbeaks, Galapagos finches, sparrows, goldfinches, crossbills, canary, bullfinches, bunting and cardinals.

Above: Most widely distributed and common of Australian finches, the Zebra Finch *(Poephila guttata)* occurs in a variety of habitats in the dry districts of every mainland State. This bird is one of the first to take advantage of rain in arid regions, at any time of the year. Rainfall is extremely erratic over most of this bird's range of distribution, but these birds are among the fastest to respond, beginning to build nests within a few hours of the commencement of heavy rain. The young grow and mature so quickly that within about four weeks they have left the nest, allowing their parents to commence a second brood. Just nine or ten weeks after hatching they themselves have full adult plumage and may commence to breed if favourable conditions still prevail. A few months of plentiful water and grass seed food are sufficient to ensure a population explosion of these finches.

Right: The splash of bright red on otherwise inconspicuous greenish plumage makes the Star Finch *(Neochmia ruficauda)* a very attractive small bird of far northern and north-western Australia. This species is generally found where the vegetation is more dense. In the spinifex country, as in the north-west, they are most often seen where rain has brought tall grass to the banks and floodplains of creeks and rivers. Typically, they will be seen in flocks of up to several hundred birds, but these break up and separate into pairs when breeding. Star Finches have elaborate courtship displays, the male singing, dancing, a long green grass stem held in his bill.

Below: The bold crimson, white and black of the Painted Firetail may be overlooked when flocks of these birds fly up from the spinifex where they feed on the seed-heads. But seen close at hand, or through binoculars in full sunlight, the bold plumage is impressive.

These birds, also known as Painted Finches, of all Australian finches are most typically birds of arid environments. Their favourite haunts are ranges with spinifex vegetation, and here they will often be seen in or near gorges where there may be pools or water. The Painted Firetail may be seen almost anywhere through the northern interior, from Queensland through the Northern Territory to north-western Australia. The bulky nest of sticks is a complex structure. Built in a clump of spinifex, of globular shape, it has a very solid base platform of quite thick sticks weighed down with earth and sometimes stones.

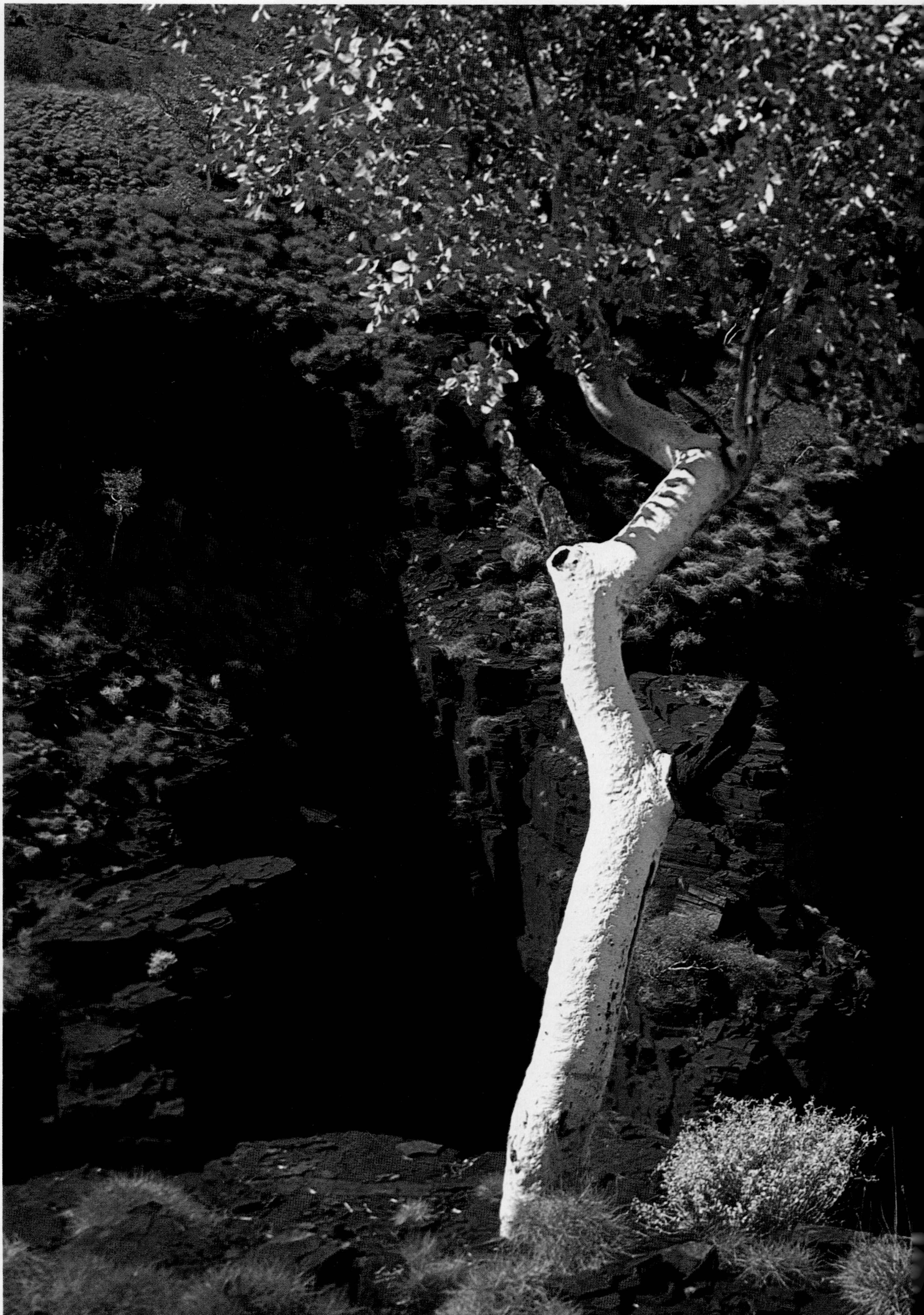

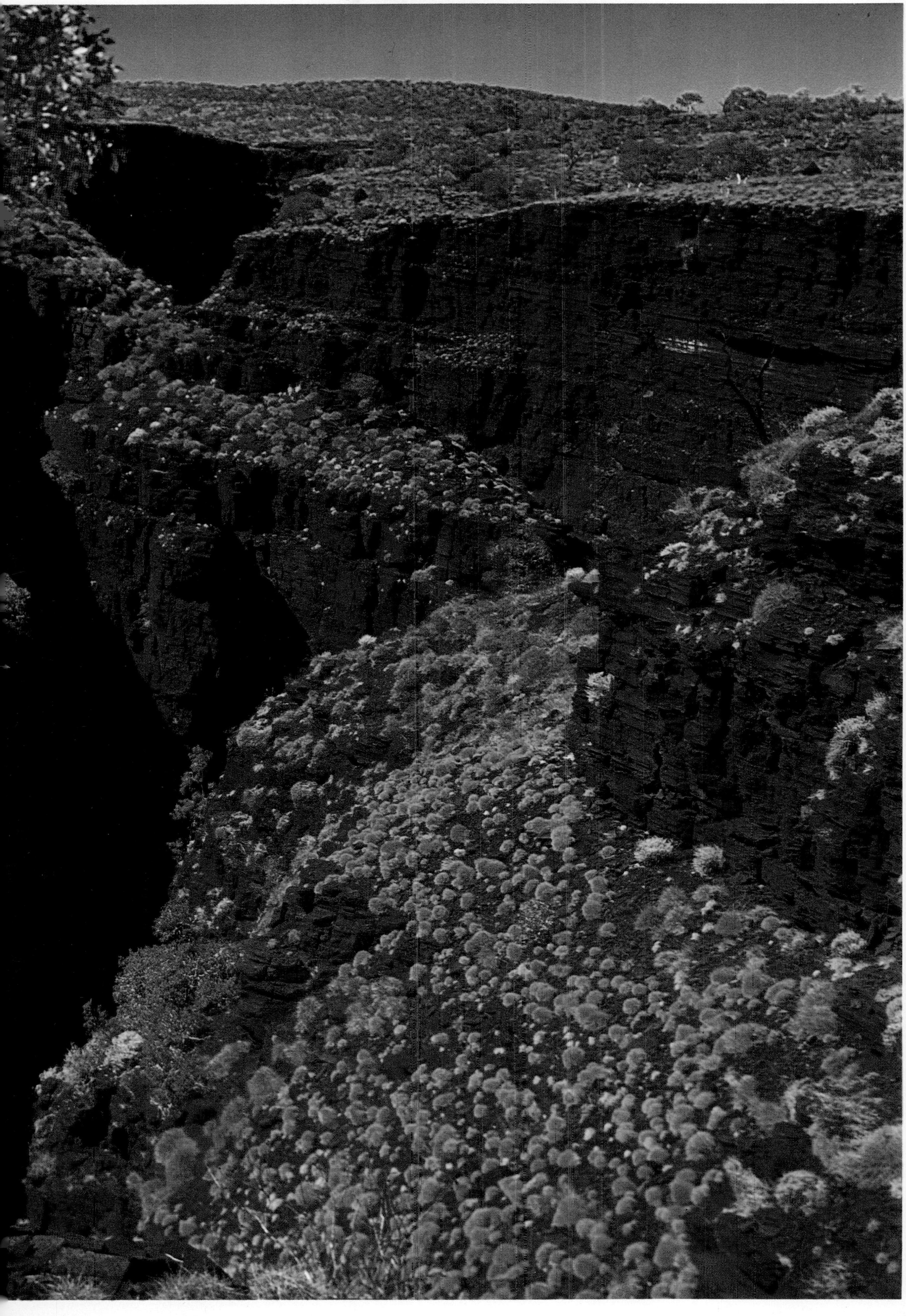

Previous page: Ranges are focal points of most arid spinifex regions. Places of bold stark beauty, they have greater concentrations of wildlife than the surrounding countryside. Along the range tops, often growing precariously from rock ledges and crevices, are small Ghost Gums, their trunks incredibly white against sky that, by contrast, seems darker blue. In this world of colour, broken rock escarpments vary from blacks and browns to bright red and rusty tones, and almost white. Rock and earth are rarely concealed by dense vegetation, for there is little more than the spinifex, that clings in little pockets of soil in the sides of ranges and gorges. The most spectacular and accessible spinifex ranges are probably the MacDonnell Ranges of the Northern Territory, and the Hamersley Ranges of Australia's far north-west.

Above: The Yellow-faced Whip-snake *(Demansia psammophis)* has a wide distribution from eastern to western coasts of Australia, but is absent from parts of far northern Australia, the south coast, and Tasmania. Perhaps as a consequence of this great variety of habitats from coastal forests to central deserts, there are many differing colour forms. These range from a uniform greyish, in south-eastern Australia, to green with dark-edged scales that form an attractive network pattern, in parts of South Australia and Western Australia. There are usually some yellowish markings on the sides of the head. The average maximum length is about 1 m; only the largest specimens are considered dangerous.

Left: The common name of Dunnart is given to about eleven species of mouse-sized insectivorous marsupials. Although superficially rather mouse-like, a second glance reveals a creature unlike any rodent mouse. The Dunnarts have sharp-pointed, alert, rather foxy little faces, large black eyes and big ears. Its teeth, unlike the flat gnawing mouse teeth, are the needle-pointed cat-like teeth of a hunter, although so small they can scarcely break through human skin. The Hairy-footed Dunnart *(Sminthopsis hirtipes)* has the pads of the soles of its feet covered with hairs, perhaps to assist in traversing the loose sand of desert dunes, for it inhabits very arid regions of the Northern Territory and central deserts of Western Australia.

Above: The Black-headed Monitor *(Varanus tristis)* is a sleek, slender, very fast-moving goanna, which preys upon lizards, mice and insects. In arid, largely treeless regions it lives in a crevice among rocks, or in a burrow, or where there are trees, in a hollow limb. There are two subspecies. This is a dark-coloured form, which inhabits arid central and western parts of the continent. A smaller northern speckled form extends from northern New South Wales through Queensland and the Northern Territory to the Kimberleys.

Right: The shrubs and small trees known as eremophilas are aptly named, for it means 'desert lovers', and most are plants of desert or semi-arid regions. The Kopi Poverty Bush *(Eremophila miniata),* in common with many of its genus, has foliage with a rather sticky resinous coating which probably reduces water loss. A shrub with a maximum height of about 4 m, the Kopi Poverty Bush grows in the interior of Western Australia, often in the vicinity of salt lakes. Most, but not all, eremophilas appear to be adapted for pollination by the honey-eating birds of the arid regions, for their flowers are often red, and of a deep tubular shape appropriate for the honeyeater bill.

Above: Commonly known as the Military Dragon, this lizard has a wide distribution across the interior of Australia. It extends from western Queensland through dry parts of the Northern Territory to South Australia into central and north-western parts of Western Australia. Many differing patterns and colours occur across great distances and variety of habitat. Distinctive sub-species are found in northern, central, western and northern areas. This species *Amphibolurus isolepis,* is a swift-running, ground-dwelling dragon lizard which feeds on insects, spiders and other small creatures it can capture. Dragon lizards belong to the family Agamidae of which about 50 species are found in Australia. All are egg-laying, and unlike snakes and geckos, they do not shed their tails in order to escape predators. The largest group within the dragon family, the genus *Amphibolurus,* is found throughout Australia. However, the greatest number of species are restricted to arid regions.

Above: A few weeks after rain, tall grass begins to conceal the harsh landscape of bare earth and the dead skeletons of drought-stricken mulga trees. These are softer grasses than the spinifex. Australia's major areas of arid tussock grasslands are in western Queensland and the eastern parts of the Northern Territory. There are broad expanses of treeless grasslands between Burketown and Normanton on the Barkly Tableland, extending westwards into the Northern Territory, and southwards into the regions of Queensland traversed by the Diamantina River and Cooper's Creek. In seasons when perennial grasses are at their most luxuriant, seed-eating birds and mammals become abundant. Flocks of Budgerigars and of various finches, and parties of parrots move in from distant regions. Native rodents increase, and soon after, so do the hawks and owls which prey upon them.

Right: Small eucalypts, dazzlingly white-barked, are scattered through the rocky spinifex country, and are usually known as 'ghost gums'. Several species may be given this common name, including *Eucalyptus leucophloia* and *Eucalyptus papuana*. At night, by the faint light of moon or stars, the white trunks and outreaching limbs of these trees stand as ghostly pale shapes against black night sky or dark gorges. Alternatively known as 'Porcupine Grass', spinifex has leaves not only needle-pointed, but also with sticky resinous surfaces. The Aborigines made use of this resin, which was beaten out, and softened by heating, to be used with bindings to attach sharp stone spear tips and axe heads to the wooden shafts. Spinifex clumps are the hiding places and homes of geckos, skinks and insects, which the Aborigines captured by burning each clump in turn.

Left: In parts of central Australia, large stately Desert Oaks grow across the spinifex plains, and in some localities are so numerous that a woodland landscape is created, in contrast to the almost treeless surrounding landscapes. The Desert Oak *(Casuarina decaisneana)* may reach a height of some 20 m, and has fine dense massed foliage. This tree appears to grow where there is deep underground water. Even the spinifex, though grass-like, has very deep-reaching roots. Although the spinifex has stiff sharp leaves, the tall seed stems are flexible and softer and on the desert plains look like vast fields of wheat; the seeds were collected by the Aborigines and ground into a kind of flour. The desert grass commonly called spinifex is of many similar species, which belong to the genera, *Triodia* with about 35 species, and *Plectrachne,* of about 10 species, both groups found only in Australia.

Left: The most distinctive feature of the Mulgara, and one which allows immediate identification, is the tail. Not long, it is thick and of reddish colour with a contrasting crest-like brush of long shining black hairs along the upper surface of its terminal half. The female Mulgara, also known as the Crest-tailed Marsupial-mouse, has about seven young, which cling beneath their mother, for although these are marsupials, a deep pouch has not evolved. The young remain clinging even while she hunts, which she seems able to do successfully even when the young have grown so large that she appears to stagger under their weight.

Above: Knob-tailed geckos are among the most fascinating of small reptiles. Big-eyed, their facial expressions seem to possess character far greater than usual for reptiles. Their response to a close approach, when they raise themselves high on stiffened legs, even arching the back cat-like and making angry sounds, also makes them rather exceptional, for most reptiles react simply by freezing, or by departing rapidly. Knob-tailed geckos have in common their most unusual tails, which are very short, usually flattened, and terminate in a peculiar round knob. This makes a weird contrast with their disproportionately big heads and huge soulful eyes. Fascinating, too, is the way in which they use their tongues in a quick windscreen-wiper action across their eyes. This Knob-tail, *Nephrurus levis*, inhabits central arid parts of all mainland states of Australia, except Victoria. By day it lives in a burrow, emerging at night to hunt on areas of open ground for insects.

TROPICAL AND TEMPERATE RAINFORESTS

The world of the rainforest is one of soft luminous light filtered through the leaves of the treetop canopy. Tall trees soar to a dense canopy shutting out almost all direct sunlight.

Probably the most striking feature of the rainforest is the gloom of its depths. Very little light penetrates the mass of vegetation high above the ground. But mature rainforest is not an impenetrable mass of vegetation. The space beneath is open, often described as cathedral-like. Massive treetrunks soar upwards through cavernous dimly-lit spaces, branching outwards far above to support a leafy screen that permits only remote glimpses of sky.

The tree foliage tends to be in two or three layers, but this is not obvious — the forest appears to be in chaotic confusion. Beneath these foliage canopies, the treetrunks are straight, with very little side branching or vegetation.

Sunlight reaches the rainforest floor in small dappled patches and even then, only in the middle of the day. Away from these sparse spots of sun, the light intensity may be less than one-hundredth that of the sunlight above the forest. Few plants can grow here, so there is rarely any shrub layer, and the ground is almost devoid of small plants. There are seedlings of the big trees overhead, but these grow so slowly that they are almost dormant, some species reaching but a metre or two after several decades. They await the death and collapse of a tree, when the light admitted by the break in the canopy will send these waiting seedlings and saplings shooting upwards, until the gap is again filled with foliage. Some plants may not be capable of surviving this long near-dormant period; it has been suggested that most species of eucalypts cannot grow in rainforest for this reason.

During the millions of years of evolution, of competing for light and mineral nutrients, many plants have adopted unusual life forms. One is the woody climbing plant, the liane. Like the trees, it begins its life in gloomy ground-level shade, but it needs higher light intensity when mature. Lianes entwine and climb the trees, frequently crossing from tree to tree, finally to reach the forest roof.

Epiphytes have solved the problem in a different way, escaping the gloom of the lower levels by germinating and growing upon the high limbs. The stranglers, too, germinate high in the forest, but soon drop many fine roots to the ground.

These thicken, enshrouding the supporting tree in a mesh of roots that at first are a fine network, but thickening become an almost solid wooden coffin within which the host tree cannot expand or grow, and in which it dies, rots, and finally leaves standing the hollow tube of the strangler.

In Australia, tropical rainforests occur down the eastern coast, from Cape York to the Richmond River area. Further south is sub-tropical rainforest, with fewer species of trees, but with epiphyte ferns and mosses more common.

The most southerly temperate rainforest is often dominated by a single species of tree, with lower levels covered in ferns, mosses and lichens. Temperate rainforest occurs in Tasmania, and extends northwards up the east coast, particularly at higher altitudes; on cool mountain tops, this vegetation reaches Northern Queensland.

Less well known are the monsoon forests of northern Australia. Monsoon forest, recognisably similar to rainforest, occurs mostly in small patches across coastal northern Australia, from north Queensland to the Kimberleys. Although accommodating many rainforest birds and other animals, monsoon forests, in areas characterised by a long dry winter between summer monsoon rains, have few of the moisture-loving epiphytes of the rainforests.

Tropical and sub-tropical rainforests can be seen in many east-coastal national parks. Some of the most accessible and impressive in north Queensland are the Palmerston National Park and the Mt. Hypipamee National Park both on the Atherton Tableland, and Eungella National Park on the Clarke Range west of Mackay. Other areas, less easily accessible, preserve rainforests on the Bellenden-Ker Range near Cairns and the Mt. Windsor Tablelands on the Upper Daintree River near Mossman, north Queensland.

On Australia's mid-east coast, in south-eastern Queensland and north-eastern New South Wales, the character of the rainforest has changed from that of the far north. Although basically similar to the tropical rainforest, these sub-tropical rainforests are less rich in plant and animal species. But there are still tropical rainforest features of plank buttresses, lianes, strangler figs and open, gloomy lower levels. There are usually more epiphytes, ferns and

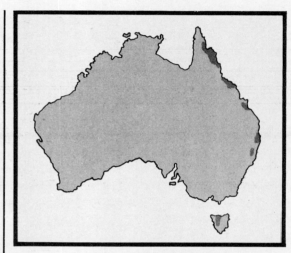

mosses in sub-tropical rainforests.

Temperate rainforest, however, is conspicuously different. There are no plank buttresses, no stout woody vines and trees of relatively few different species intermingled.

Many of the national parks of the central eastern coast contain both sub-tropical rainforest, on the lower eastern slopes of the ranges, and temperate rainforest at high altitudes. Well-known are Lamington National Park of south-eastern Queensland, and New England National Park of north-eastern New South Wales.

But the cool temperate rainforests are best seen in western Tasmania, on the mountain slopes, which receive not warm tropical downpours but cold blustery gales from the Southern Ocean, often with snowfalls even in summer.

These areas possess some of the most interesting rainforests. Trails around Cradle Mountain and from Lake St. Clair on to nearby mountains lead into fascinating rainforest totally unlike that of the tropical north. The Antarctic Beech tree dominates these forests, together with some King Villy Pine and Celery-top Pine. Beneath occur some small shrubs, including the palm-like *Richea pandanifolia*. The most striking feature is the totally green appearance beneath the forest canopy.

Opposite page: In their dimly lit greenery, the rainforests which cover the lower slopes of Tasmanian mountains resemble tropical rainforests. However, they have fewer tree species, and mosses and ferns dominate the lower levels. This temperate rainforest is on the lower slopes of Mt. Olympus, beside Lake St. Clair.

Left: The Pale-yellow Robin *(Eopsaltria capito)* is one of a group of Australian yellow-breasted robins, but its yellow is slightly paler, and of more greenish-yellow colour. This bird has a broken distribution. One population inhabits coastal rainforests of south-eastern Queensland and north-eastern New South Wales, while a second separate population, a slightly different sub-species, occurs in north-eastern Queensland in the rainforests between Cooktown and Townsville. This bird seems to favour rainforest areas where the spiny lawyer vine occurs, which is often used as a site for the neat and well-camouflaged nest.

Right: The Tiger Cat is by far the largest of Australia's four species of native cats, and the one species in which white spots of the coat extend on to the tail. None of these animals are really cats, nor are they at all related to the feline cats. But there are few other appropriate descriptive names for an animal which is cat-like in its nocturnal hunting skills. The Tiger Cat has a reputation for fearlessness and ferocity that earns the tiger comparison. It is the largest tree-climbing marsupial carnivore, said to be able to take quite large prey, even very small wallabies. The Tiger Cat inhabits dense forests, heavy scrubs and rainforests of the coasts and ranges of eastern Queensland, eastern New South Wales, southern Victoria and the south-east of South Australia. Tasmania is probably its stronghold.

Left: Growing on rainforest trees from northern New South Wales to north-eastern Queensland, the King Orchid *(Dendrobium speciosum)* forms bulky clumps with long racemes of bright yellow flowers, seen high in the sunlit upper strata of the rainforests. A very slightly different sub-species known as the Rock Orchid, makes similar epiphytic clumps on bare rock outcrops of the humid parts of eastern coastal Australia, from Victoria to northern Queensland. Individual flowers, growing on long racemes, are up to 5 cm across.

Above: One of Australia's most spectacular birds for plumage, the Regent Bowerbird *(Sericulus chrysocephalus)* when flying through the gloomy rainforests looks like a huge golden butterfly: yellow patches on beating wings clearly visible, but the black plumage almost lost against the dark shadowy background. This bowerbird, known also as the Regent-bird, occurs along the mid-east coast of Australia in the rainforests of north-eastern New South Wales, and Queensland as far north as Mackay. The bower built by the male is a twin-walled avenue of sticks, like that of the Satin bowerbird, but smaller.

Left: The rainforests along the coastal ranges of eastern Queensland contain a world of contrasts. Shafts of brilliant sunlight burst through gaps in the overhead foliage canopy, and highlight the bright greens of epiphytic ferns, and mossy trunks. All around the detail of the lower levels is lost in the gloomy half-light.

Right: In north-eastern Queensland, around Cairns, Innisfail and the Atherton Tableland, anyone visiting one of the national parks, following one of the walk tracks through gloomy rainforest, may find himself confronting this incredible reptile. Greenish colours, and rows of white spines make Boyd's Forest Dragon quite startling close at hand. The habit of remaining motionless on a treetrunk, colours blending with mossy bark, means that this reptile is often not noticed until almost within touching distance. But despite its appearance, Boyd's Forest Dragon *(Gonocephalus boydii)* is completely harmless, and seems to rely upon camouflage for protection. Australia has two, possibly three species of the forest dragons of this genus, which is centred mainly upon the tropical rainforests of South-east Asia, Malaysia and New Guinea.

Flying into its nest tunnel in a creek bank, an Azure Kingfisher, its swift flight frozen by high-speed photography, shows detail of action that otherwise would be too swift to appreciate. Familiar though the shape and plumage of this bird may be when perched, it is for the function of flight that its plumage, and indeed, almost the entire form of its body, have evolved. Only in flight do the wonderfully designed wings and tail come into action, with every feather playing a vital part in the speed and incredible control of the bird in the air. A kingfisher perched reveals little of its ability to dash at speed along a narrow creek, around curves, beneath logs and overhanging banks, between rocks and reeds, through gaps in foliage, skimming the water surface, so fast that it can be hard for the eye to follow. At this speed the kingfisher approaches the small round hole in the creek bank, the entrance to its nest tunnel. Just when it seems that the bird cannot possibly slow in time to avoid violent impact, it applies parachute-like air breaks, and makes a gentle, perfectly controlled and natural landing just inside the narrow tunnel opening. In that last instant it turns its entire body to a vertical position in the air, spreading wings and tail against cushioning air, then, its speed greatly slowed, folds its wings to drop into the tunnel entrance. Only by high-speed photographic techniques, with action-

stopping exposures of one ten-thousandth of a second, can the incredible skill of a small bird in flight be studied, and the functional beauty of its plumage appreciated. The Azure Kingfisher *(Ceyx azurea)* is an inhabitant of eastern coastal parts of New South Wales and Queensland, south-eastern parts of South Australia, and the entire States of Victoria and Tasmania. It extends across coastal northern Australia to the Kimberleys. The Azure Kingfisher keeps to waterways, but may be seen in habitats of considerably diversity; ranging from creeks of rainforests or open woodlands, to mangrove swamps, or coastal estuaries. It is most often noticed perched on a branch overhanging the water, watching for movement below, when it will dive bill-first into the water, to emerge with a small fish or other aquatic creature.

Previous page: Storm clouds conceal the summit of the Bellenden-Ker Range, Queensland's highest mountain. Tropical rainforests cover its lower slopes, extending from the Russell River on the coastal plains to its 1500 m summit. Vegetation and animal life change with increasing altitude. On the lowlands are palm forests, and birds found only at lower altitudes, such as the White-tailed Kingfisher. At higher altitudes are native rhododendrons, Golden Bowerbirds, and Green Ringtail Possums.

Left: One of a comparatively few honeyeaters inhabiting rainforests, the Lewin Honeyeater *(Meliphaga lewini)* is a species that has diversified in its foraging habits, feeding on soft fruits such as paw paws, as well as the native fruits of the forests. At times these birds have been seen spiralling up the trunks and limbs like treecreepers, searching for insects in bark crevices. The Lewin Honeyeater tends to prefer the rainforests of mountainous regions, specifically from north-eastern Queensland through eastern New South Wales to south-eastern Victoria. The plumage of this honeyeater blends well with the universal greenery of the rainforests, the only bright parts being the yellow ear tufts; male and female are alike in their plumage.

Above: Found only in the rainforests and dense wet eucalypt forests of north-eastern New South Wales and south-eastern Queensland, the Rufous Scrub-bird *(Atrichornis rufescens)* is one of Australia's rare birds, and is not easily seen. In the dense tangled forest-floor vegetation and debris it creeps, mouse-like and hidden, rarely flying. Its presence may be revealed by its extremely loud, resonant calls. The Rufous Scrub-bird is strongly territorial, but its territories seem widely dispersed. The female alone builds the nest, which is very well concealed close to the ground in dense vegetation.

Left: In the tropical rainforests fascinating treetop gardens are constructed by ferns and epiphytic orchids. A species of the latter, the Orange-blossom Orchid *(Sarcochilus falcatus),* has large flowers, which hang in multiple racemes, and are highly perfumed under the morning sun.

Left: Among the most typical of the sounds of the coastal and mountain rainforests of New South Wales and south-eastern Queensland are those of the Green Cat-bird *(Ailuroedus crassirostris).* These resemble a loud cat-like mewing, or the wailing of a baby. At other times this bird makes clicking noises. Rainforest fruits and seeds are the usual food. The Green Cat-bird builds an open cup-shaped nest, well-hidden in a tangle of vines or other dense clump of rainforest vegetation. Australia has a second species, the Spotted Cat-bird, similar in general appearance to the Green Cat-bird, but smaller. It is confined to far north-eastern Queensland, and is the sub-species of a New Guinea cat-bird; like the Green Cat-bird, the spotted variety is a rainforest inhabitant.

Left: Green Tree Ants of Northern Australia cannot be overlooked. In very close-up detail these ants are beautifully coloured, bright translucent green. Usually trees with large broad leaves are favoured for their nests. To watch the teamwork of the Green Tree Ants *(Oecophylla virescens)* is fascinating. The ants form living chains from one leaf to the next, and by combined strength pull the leaves together until their edges touch. Then other workers appear from within the nest carrying ant larvae. Unlike the adults, these can produce silk, which they produce to spin cocoons in which to pupate. When held to the junction between the leaves, the larvae join the leaves with their sticky silk, making a strong and waterproof nest.

Above: Palm forests grow in the deep valleys of Dorrigo National Park, on the mountain slopes of north-eastern New South Wales. Here the Bangalow Palm (*Archontophoenix cunninghamiana*) grows along the Little North Arm of the Bellinger River, where there are deep alluvial soils and high rainfall. This rainforest is dense and luxuriant, a well preserved remnant of the sub-tropical rainforest that once covered much of this region but has now been cleared for dairying. Huge buttressed trees grow along the trails, including Red Cedar, Coachwoods, Giant Stinging Trees, Illawarra Flame Trees and Yellow Carabeens. This rainforest habitat shelters many species of birds and mammals native to rainforests, including Brush Turkeys, Regent and Satin Bowerbirds, and Lyrebirds.

Right: Hartz Mountain is a glacier-carved plateau in southern Tasmania, and rises to an altitude of 1254 m. Numerous small lakes lie in ice-gouged hollows on the plateau-top, and overflow to tumble down the mountainside into forests below. The cold waters of this unnamed waterfall cascade through a deep ravine of glistening black boulders, into fern gullies, rainforests and wet sclerophyll forests. From the top of the Hartz Mountains, above these falls, there are views over rugged terrain into the wild south-west of the island.

Left: A very long slender snake, the Green Tree Snake is widespread in forested northern and eastern coastal parts of Australia. This snake is able to climb swiftly through shrubbery and into trees. There are numerous colour variations, the most common in eastern Australia being green above, yellow beneath, but including some that are black above and yellow below, and occasional individuals entirely blue. Those from the far north-west are often entirely yellow and are commonly known by the name Golden Tree Snake. The Green Tree Snake, *Dendrelaphis punctulatus,* sometimes called the Common Tree Snake, grows to a length of about 2 m, and is not venomous.

Right: Temperate rainforest clothes the higher parts of the Great Dividing Range. At New England National Park this rainforest extends down the slopes to about 1000 m altitude, and has a mysterious atmosphere, its ancient great trees shrouded with mosses and lichens. Some of the trees here are estimated to be three thousand years old. This Antarctic Beech *(Nothogagus moorei)* occurs also in Tasmania, New Zealand and South America. It is part of the evidence for the theory that these land masses were once joined together. This beech is not a relic, but is a normal forest of Australia's highest eastern mountain tops, where there is a rainfall of around 250 mm annually, and frequent summer mists.

Right: A Tree Frog *(Hyla peroni)* of coastal eastern Australia displays fantastic marbled eyes with peculiarly angular pupils. Tiny flecks of bright emerald green on its pale mottled skin give this frog a remarkable resemblance to the light-coloured, moss-speckled trunks of many rainforest trees. Frogs of the family Hylidae are characterized by the suction discs on the ends of their fingers and toes, giving a sure grip on smooth branch and leaf surfaces. The male frog has a throat (or gular) pouch, which can be inflated with air from the lungs, and acts as a resonator in croaking. This species gives a high-pitched, prolonged croak.

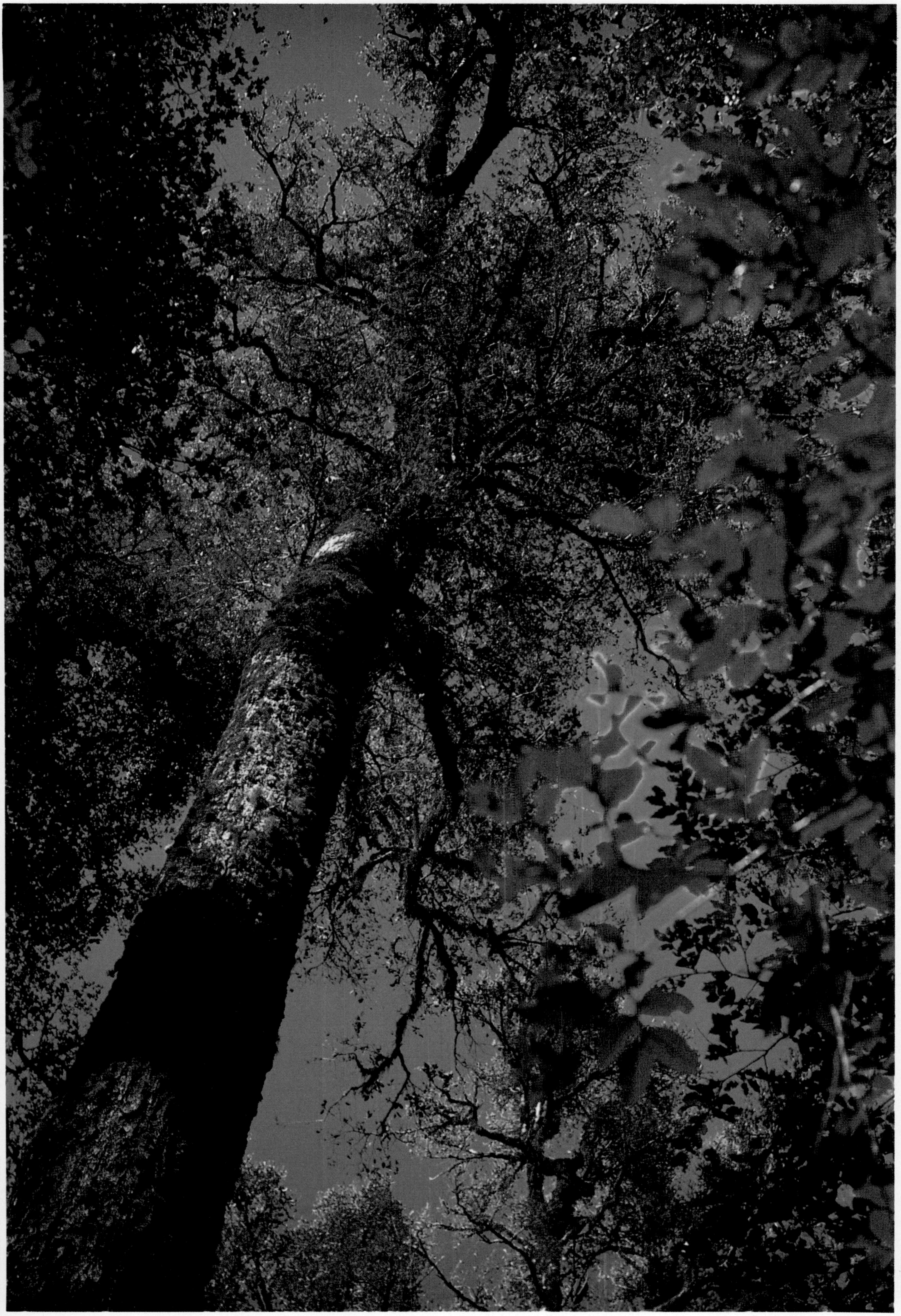

Above: The Mountain Brushtail must be one of the most attractive of the large possums, with big bulging brown eyes, and a face that seems to carry a permanent expression of surprise. The fur is luxuriant, with a silvery sheen. Unlike the Common Brushtail, a very common animal in the city suburbs, living in house roofs and completely adapting to the man-made environment, the Mountain Brushtail is a shy animal of rainforests. It would almost certainly vanish wherever its habitat is damaged or adversely disturbed. This possum *(Trichosurus caninus)* occurs in eastern Australia, from southern Queensland to Victoria.

Right: The bower of the Satin Bowerbird *(Ptilonorhynchus violaceus)* consists of two walls of vertical sticks. During the spring months the gleaming male almost constantly attends the bower, adjusting the sticks of the walls, arranging the decorations of flowers, snail shells, native fruits, flowers and mosses, and even painting the walls a brownish colour with natural pigments using a brush of bark fibres. The Satin Bowerbird inhabits rainforest and adjacent wet sclerophyll forests, of two geographic areas. A southern population inhabits coastal ranges of south-eastern Australia, from the Gladstone and Bunya Mountains area of Queensland, to the Otway Ranges of Victoria. The second population is on the high ranges of north-eastern Queensland, from Townsville to Cooktown. There are probably about 19 species of bowerbirds, 6 occurring only in Australia, 11 only in New Guinea, and 2 common to both Australia and New

Guinea. Most inhabit regions of mountains and tropical rainforests. In Australia, by way of contrast, several species live in semi-desert country.

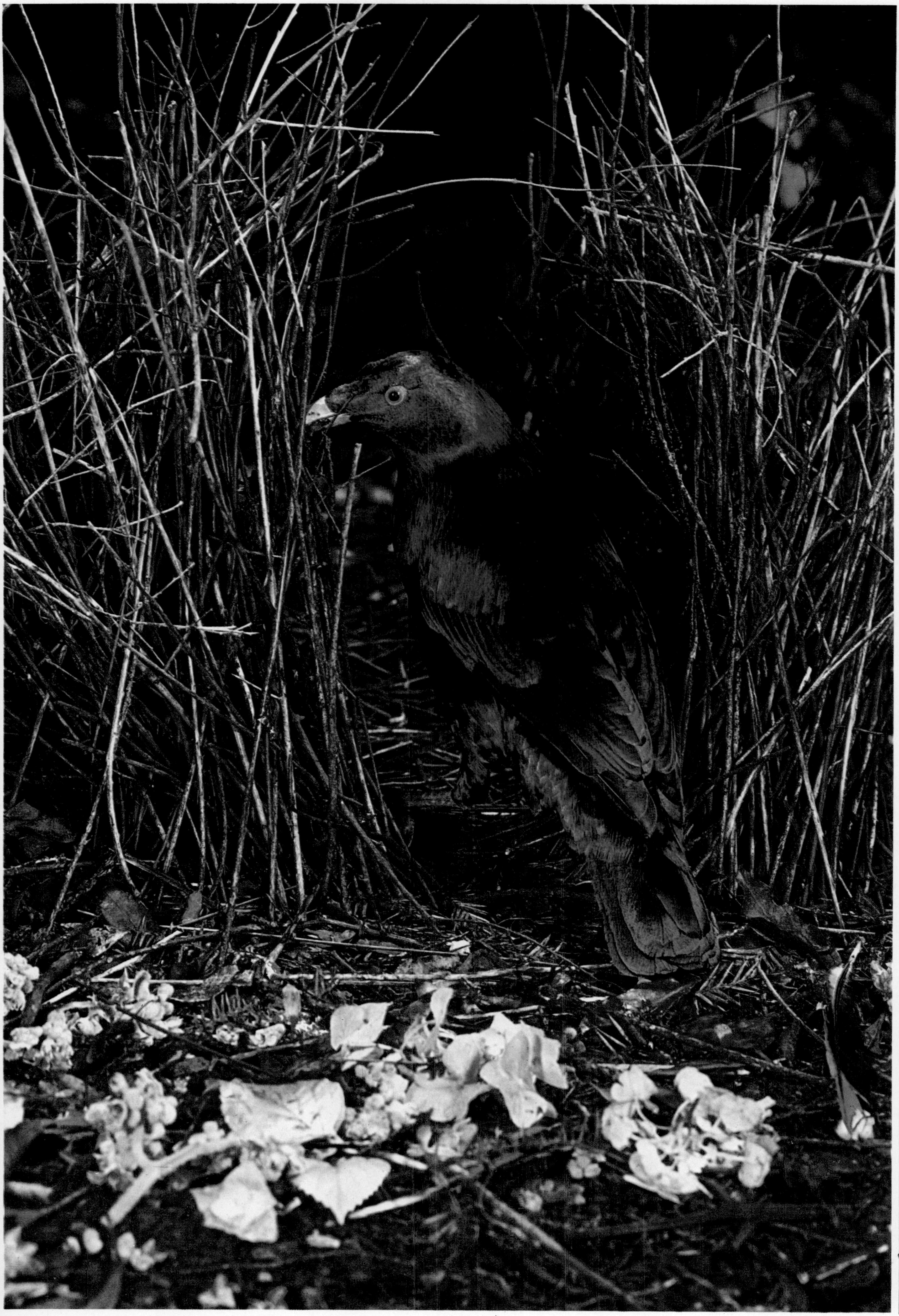

Left: Though dissimilar to rainforests of tropical north-eastern Australia, the rainforests of south-western Tasmania share an overwhelming abundance of plant life. The trunks of trees, logs and stumps in this the wettest part of Tasmania, are totally covered with mosses, fungi, lichens and small ferns, particularly on their shaded southern surfaces. The bark or dead wood may be totally hidden. The ground also is completely concealed by ferns and mosses, and the sky almost blocked out by the screen of overhead foliage. The birds of these Tasmanian rainforests are not of a great many species, but include the Olive Whistler, Eastern Spinebill, Pink Robin, Green Rosella, Ground Thrush, and Scrub-wren, and unique to Tasmania, the Scrub-tit and the Tasmanian Thornbill.

Right: The Golden Bowerbird is found only in mountainous rainforests of north-eastern Queensland. Although it is the smallest of the Australian bowerbirds, this species *(Prionodura newtoniana)* builds the largest display bower. This is of the 'maypole' style of construction, a contrast to the avenue shape used by other Australian bowerbirds. Two towers of sticks rise almost 2 m in height, and are joined by a horizontal display perch which is decorated with golden-green lichens and yellow flowers of jungle orchids. The bower is used for many seasons, becoming more massive as the years pass. This bower is the 'focal point' of the bird's territory, to which the calling, displaying male attracts the females. The male, his energies devoted to attending the bower, takes no part in the nest-building or feeding of the young. After mating at the bower, the females construct a nest tucked into a hollow or ledges on the side of a treetrunk in dense rainforest.

Above: The Pearly-winged Flycatcher *(Monarcha melanopsis)* is a bird of the coastal forests and occasionally of woodlands, where it captures insects on the foliage. The nest of this bird, also known as the Black-faced Flycatcher, is a beautifully constructed cup of mosses blended on to the branch. This bird is a member of the group known as the Monarch Flycatchers. The Pearly-winged Flycatcher may be seen in coastal forests of eastern Australia, from north-eastern Queensland through eastern New South Wales, as far as south-eastern Victoria.

Right: Known as the Red-eyed Tree Frog, the species *Litoria rothi* is an inhabitant of the vegetation of the margins of swamps and streams of the tropical northern coast and northern river systems. Its distribution extends from eastern Queensland through the Northern Territory to the Kimberley region. The colour of this frog varies from almost white to grey-brown.

MULGA AND OTHER ACACIA SCRUBLANDS

In Australia, probably more than any other habitat, the mulga is transformed almost beyond recognition by the extremes of the seasons. The touch of rain upon land parched and heated for months or years, receives full recognition through an explosion of life and colour. The effect of rain is dramatically shown in the cycle of growth that it triggers.

Except perhaps in some coastal regions which have a reliable rainfall throughout the year, the bush responds to rain after any lengthy dry spell with a fresh burst of life. The extent to which this occurs, the degree to which it is visibly displayed, depends upon the way in which the life-cycle of each of its living things, plant and animal, is evolved to respond to rain.

Spinifex country will change in overall appearance from gold to green, and small wildflowers appear between the hummocks. Some regions of mallee scrub will, after rain, have many flowers on trees and shrubs, but other mallee scrubs have a ground stratum so densely littered with twig and leaf debris that there are relatively few small plants even after rain. In tropical woodland, the wet season storms bring a lush growth of green, as tall grasses conceal the dusty earth of the dry season. These are indeed expressions of the changing seasons. But it is in mulga scrub that one of the most impressive visual transformations occurs.

In the semi-arid mulga country a prolonged period of drought, even just one summer without rain, can create a landscape that seems one of hopeless loss of all life that could be sustained either on, or in, the land. The only vegetation is of a few sparsely scattered mulga trees and shrubs, looking wizened, almost lifeless. The ground is barren, without the touch of green of small plants, whether it be rocky, or hard-baked clay, or loose red dust.

By contrast, the mulga scrub in early spring, several months after good winter rains, can present a carpet of massed flowers extending, as it were, endlessly for hundreds of kilometres along the roadside, covering millions of hectares. Because there are few small shrubs near the ground, the uniform carpet-like spread of flowers is all the more conspicuous.

The ephemeral plants are almost entirely responsible for this transformation. These are short-lived herbaceous plants, soft-leaved, soft-stemmed, and without any ability to withstand the normal environment of arid heat. They have their brief few weeks of spectacular life when this near-desert country for a short time is moist, the heat less fierce. In this time they must grow to maturity, flower, and scatter their seeds. It will be a year, perhaps even five or ten, before these seeds are all germinated by the soaking rain needed to make another such impressive massed display. A light sprinkling of rain will simply produce a few sparsely scattered flowers. Most of the seeds can be awakened only by the heavy rain and soaking wetness that signals a good season for Australia's mulga scrublands.

Most of the ephemeral wildflowers are of the family Compositae, with papery flowers of pink, yellow or white, that retain a fresh appearance weeks after they have been picked, and are therefore called 'everlastings'.

Australia's semi-arid regions include vast tracts of scrub which in some areas is dense enough to produce an almost continuous low foliage canopy. But in most areas, scrub is more sparsely scattered. The mulga scrub is composed mostly of stunted trees and large shrubs of the genus *Acacia,* and like the better known coastal wattles, these too bear fluffy golden flowers, though not usually in large masses on such sparsely foliaged straggly trees. The individual trees are called 'mulgas', and the country which they dominate is known as 'the mulga'. Although most mulga trees look superficially alike, there are many species, so that the mulga scrub has variations, from one region to another, and certain of the species have local names, such as Witchetty Brush, Gidgee, Lancewood.

In central Queensland a large tract of less arid country is dominated by 'Brigalow', a dense taller scrub composed of many different trees, among which acacias are common.

The acacias of the inland, like most acacias, do not have true leaves. Rather they use phyllodes to function as leaves in the process of photosynthesis. Phyllodes are leaf stalks, which on some species may be still rounded and stalk-shaped, often stiff and with deadly sharp spine point. Others may be flattened and look like an ordinary leaf. The survival advantage is that the phyllode, like stems, is more woody in structure, able to resist wilting in hot, dry conditions, and the breathing openings, the stomata, are fewer, resulting in less moisture loss.

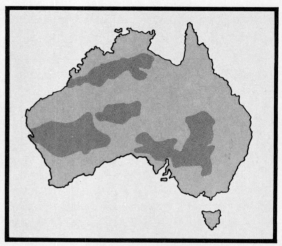

Mulga scrub occurs from the interior of Queensland and New South Wales, across central and northern parts of South Australia, to the mid-western coast of Western Australia. This habitat is readily seen along most routes through the interior of Australia.

Some of the largest reserves containing mulga, are South Australia's un-named conservation park in the far north-west corner of that State, and the Elliot Price Wilderness Conservation Park beside Lake Eyre. Queensland's Dipperu National Park reserves a segment of Brigalow and Belah scrubs. Most of the National Parks of the central Australian portion of the Northern Territory contain areas of arid mulga country.

Opposite page: Even while massed mulga wildflowers reach their peak, dark storm clouds threaten further rain. In dark outline against the sky are two *Acacia,* mulga trees. The wildflowers in this display near Alice Springs are the Tall Yellowtop *(Senecio magnificus)* and White Everlastings *(Helipterum floribundum).*

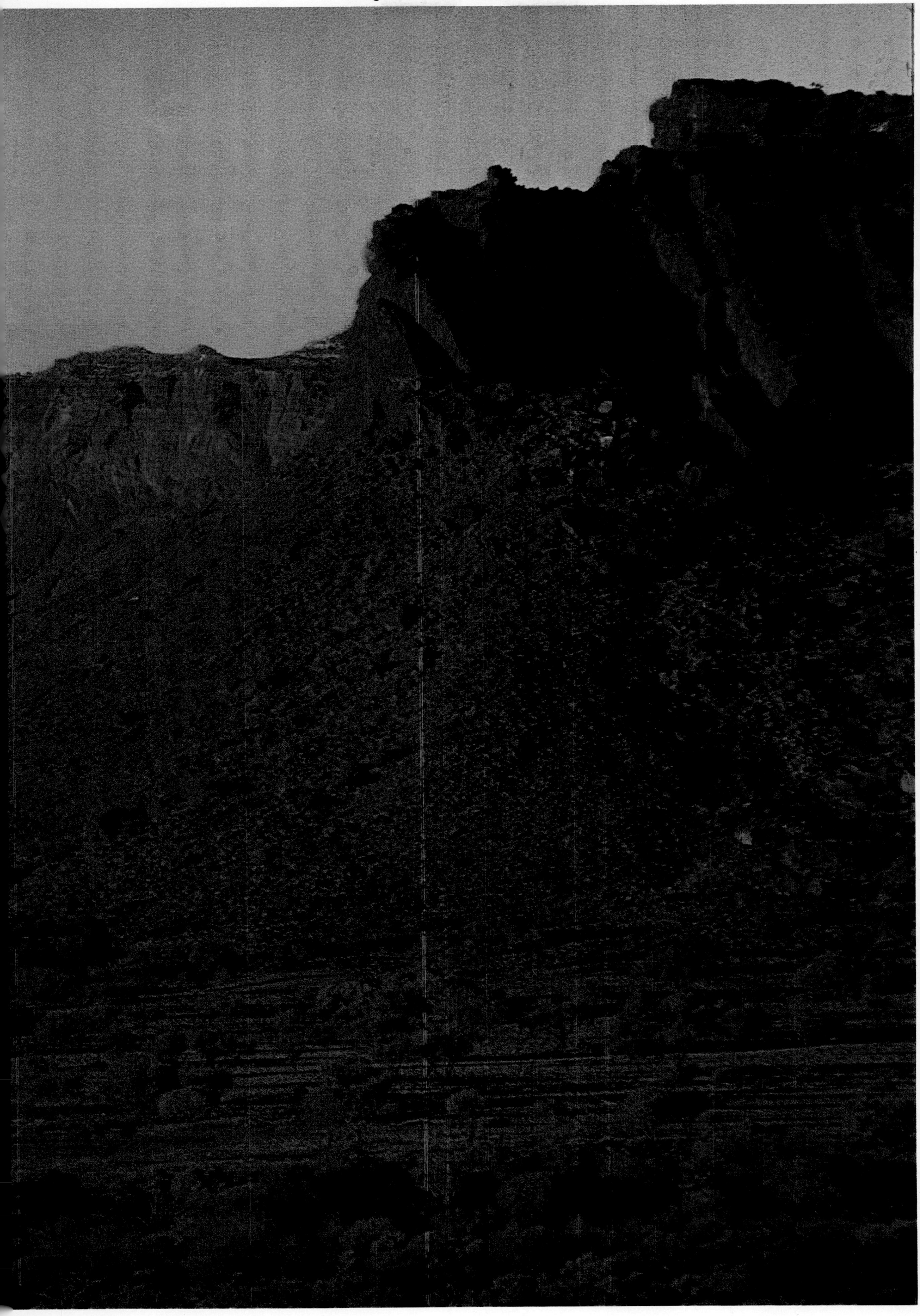

Previous page: The cliffs of this range divide two distinctly different habitats. In the heavy red clay soils of the plains below is mulga scrub, and on the flat plateau top above, sand dunes with spinifex. Each has its own wildlife, the spinifex having Rufous-crowned Emu-wrens and Hopping-mice, the mulga scrub its Red-capped Robins, White-fronted Chats, Crimson Chats, and Mulga Parrots. These east-facing cliffs of the Kennedys, in Australia's far north-west, catch the first light of sunrise, their warm-toned rock glowing above plains still dark with shadows.

Right: The Pygmy Spiny-tailed Skink *(Egernia depressa)* is a small lizard of the arid regions of central Western Australia and parts of the Northern Territory. Groups of these skinks are often to be found in the large termite mounds typical of those regions, or in tree hollows, or rock crevices. This insect-eating species reaches a maximum length of about 15 cm. The skinks of the genus *Egernia* are viviparous, that is, they do not lay eggs, but bear live young, up to six in number. Most species are active during daylight hours. However, some desert species, presumably to avoid the extreme heat, are on the move in pre-dawn and evening semi-darkness.

Right: Flying from its nest hollow, a male Mulga Parrot *(Psephotus varius)* reveals patterns and colours of plumage that are not visible when the bird is perched with wings folded. The Mulga Parrot is a bird of arid woodlands and mulga scrubs of western New South Wales, south-western Queensland, north-western Victoria, through South Australia and the Northern Territory into Western Australia. Mulga Parrots are nomadic, wandering to regions where seeds and water are available. A deep narrow hollow of a tree is chosen for a nest, and the four to six white eggs are laid on the wood dust at the bottom of the hollow. The Mulga Parrot is one of a group of four species making up the genus *Psephotus*.

Left: Widespread in arid parts of New South Wales, Queensland, South Australia, the Northern Territory and Western Australia, the tall Mulla Mulla *(Ptilotus exaltatus)* in good seasons grows rapidly to a height of as much as 1½ m. It quickly completes its life cycle and dies as the land again becomes dry and hot.

Left: Most of Australia's robins are birds of moist coastal forests, but several occur through the arid central Australian regions. The Red-capped Robin *(Petroica goodenovii)* is characteristically a bird of arid regions, but also occurs in dry woodlands, mallee and open forests. Almost throughout the dry mulga scrublands of the interior, the cheery ticking trill of the Red-capped Robin is one of the most familiar of sounds. The nest of this robin is a beautifully constructed cup of bark and grass, bound with cobwebs, and clad on the outside with small pieces of bark, moss and lichens, so that the nest is blended on to the branch, and difficult to see. This bird is well adapted to the arid environment.

Below: The ground-dwelling Chestnut-breasted Quail-thrush *(Cinclosoma castanotum)* has plumage in camouflage colours and patterns to blend with the colours of its habitat. This consists of rocky hills in mulga or arid woodland country. The male has stronger colour patterns than the female, shown here on the nest. This species, of which there are several regional variations of slightly differing colour patterns, occurs in parts of western New South Wales, extending through South Australia and the southern parts of the Northern Territory into Western Australia. These birds keep to the ground, feeding on insects and seeds. When approached in the nest, in this case in a slight hollow in the ground between boulders, the sitting bird will slip off and walk inconspicuously away.

Left: On the mulga scrub plains the dead trees stand starkly against red earth and ranges, crisp white sun-bleached branches a contrast against the deep blue of clear inland skies. The mood of the arid mulga scrublands is not always pleasant. Drought is the most frequent prevailing mood, broken only seldom and briefly by the chance arrival of rain. Although the mulga scrub is well adapted to survive long rainless periods, the harsh environment takes its toll, and in most regions there are always many dead mulga trees scattered among others that show that they still have life by their sparse leaves.

Below: The Rabbit-eared Bandicoot is one of the most graceful of Australian native animals, moving with a flowing graceful motion, white-tipped tail held high like a banner. Its fur is soft, fine and silken, and its general disposition remarkably placid. In size, it is somewhat larger than an ordinary rabbit, about 70 cm from nose to tail tip. These bandicoots, also known as the Dalgytes or Bilbies, live in a warren of burrows, the tunnels of which are blocked at intervals by barriers of soft earth, possibly as barricades or to keep the interior cooler and more humid. The Rabbit-eared Bandicoot *(Macrotis lagotis)* once had a wide distribution in western New South Wales, south-western Queensland, northern South Australia, and much of Western Australia, but is now found only in some remote regions.

Left and far left: Although not colourful, the male White-fronted Chat has neat black-and-white plumage that makes him quite attractive. Also known as the White-faced Chat, this species *(Ephthianura auifrons)* is to be seen in a wide range of habitats across southern Australia. Usually this is a rather open environment such as blue-bush and saltbush plains, heaths, salt flats and dry southern mulga scrub country. White-fronted Chats occur in New South Wales, Victoria, Tasmania and South Australia and the southern half of Western Australia. These birds and the more colourful Orange Chat and Crimson Chat, are nomadic, seeking the most favourable conditions over great distances, and breeding wherever sufficient rain has fallen to bring up temporary but lush vegetation.

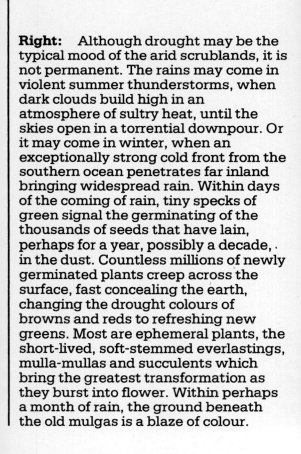

Right: Although drought may be the typical mood of the arid scrublands, it is not permanent. The rains may come in violent summer thunderstorms, when dark clouds build high in an atmosphere of sultry heat, until the skies open in a torrential downpour. Or it may come in winter, when an exceptionally strong cold front from the southern ocean penetrates far inland bringing widespread rain. Within days of the coming of rain, tiny specks of green signal the germinating of the thousands of seeds that have lain, perhaps for a year, possibly a decade, in the dust. Countless millions of newly germinated plants creep across the surface, fast concealing the earth, changing the drought colours of browns and reds to refreshing new greens. Most are ephemeral plants, the short-lived, soft-stemmed everlastings, mulla-mullas and succulents which bring the greatest transformation as they burst into flower. Within perhaps a month of rain, the ground beneath the old mulgas is a blaze of colour.

Far left: An iridescent green beetle on the clay of inland Australia resembles an emerald set in red rock, but carries the unflattering name of 'Stink Beetle'. Probably this beetle, scientifically called *Calosoma schayeri,* has no need of camouflage with its very hard carapace, and its common name suggests it is hardly likely to be the favoured prey of bird or reptile.

Left: A wolf spider *(Lycosa sp)* at night hunts with her brood of tiny spiderlings clustered all over her body. This wolf spider seemed disturbed, holding her body high above the ground, and was reluctant to return to her burrow. Investigation of her trapdoor burrow nearby showed it to have been taken over by a very large centipede, which the spider had somehow escaped.

Right: Likely to be found almost anywhere in Australia except Victoria, Tasmania and southernmost parts of New South Wales, South Australia and Western Australia, the Red-naped Snake is too small to be considered dangerous. It will, however, often bluff by striking in the manner of the large venomous snakes. The Red-naped Snake, known as *Farina diadema,* hides by day in crevices or under debris, or in ant or termite nests, emerging at night to hunt for small lizards and insects.

Left: Suddenly the red-brown landscape is lost beneath the carpeting of papery flowers, and transformed to bright yellow, pink, white or violet. By far the majority of the flowers are 'everlastings', so-called because each flower head is a composite structure of hundreds of tiny pin-head sized flowers encircled by stiff papery petal-like bracts, which do not wilt when picked. These wildflowers appear only when sufficient rain has fallen to ensure their complete growth, flowering and seeding cycle. They are able to remain impervious to any light rain that would be insufficient to see them through.

Right: The small gecko, *Diplodactylus pulcher* has an extremely variable colour pattern, which may be brown above with a pale, dark-edged back stripe, or with pale uneven patterns in place of the stripe. It may be found over a wide variety of habitats in southern and central parts of Western Australia. The twenty-two species of *Diplodactylus* comprise Australia's largest genus of geckos, and all species are unique to mainland Australia.

Right: Australia's largest goanna, sometimes more than 2½ m long, with massive body and heavy tail, the Perentie has a loose baggy-looking skin responsible for an even more formidable dinosaur-like appearance. Despite its size it is shy and at the first sign of danger will either run, to climb a tree if necessary, or lie flat and remain motionless. Its retreat is a burrow usually among rocks on a hill or ridge, or a rock crevice. The Perentie inhabits arid central regions, from western Queensland through South Australia, the Northern Territory to the north-west coast of Western Australia.

Left: The tough old mulgas are finally brought down, their hard wood hollowed, weakened, and eventually recycled to the earth by termites which everywhere are the most prolific of creatures. Although so many die, the mulga as a type of habitat, continues, as long as there are new mulga seedlings to replace the old trees that die. But in many regions this is not happening. Small new plants are quickly eaten by sheep, leaving the ground almost devoid of low small cover. Much of Australia's mulga country is undergoing a gradual but steady decline, from semi-arid scrubland towards total desert.

Above: Australia has but one species of wild dog, which is also its only large land predator that is not a marsupial, and the only member of the canine family. Elsewhere in the world the canines — cats, dogs, and other flesh-eating mammals — dominate the predatory role. But they did not reach this isolated country to displace the more ancient marsupial predators, the Tasmanian Tiger, the Tasmanian Devil, and the native-cats. In the past, Australia has had larger flesh-eating marsupials, such as the Thylacoleo or 'marsupial lion'. The Dingo can only just be considered one of Australia's native mammals, for it is a comparatively recent arrival from islands to the north, probably being brought here as a domesticated dog by the Aborigines who came via that route. Since that time the Dingo has spread throughout the continent, except in Tasmania. Australia's wild dog is not easily distinguished from many ordinary dogs of similar size except by a number of minor factors combined. The ears are always erect, the tail is bushy, the canine teeth average somewhat larger, it utters yelps and howls instead of barking, and there are some differences in basic patterns of behaviour. Colour is extremely variable, most commonly tawny yellow, with paler belly, white tail tip and feet. The earliest explorers, pushing far into regions never seen by Europeans, recorded sightings of dingos of a variety of colours.

TROPICAL FORESTS AND WOODLANDS

Few places anywhere in Australia could have equalled the intense confusion of activity of the West Kimberley woodlands in May. In full flower, the tall Darwin Woollybutt trees became a mass of deep orange, the typical eucalypt flowers massed together in great clusters. In every tree, in almost every clump of flowers, birds busily sought nectar, or insects.

Among the most conspicuous were the noisy, brilliantly colourful Red-collared Lorikeets, and the smaller Varied Lorikeets, but there seemed countless others. Harsh calls attracted attention to Silver-crowned Friar-birds, bold colours of Blue-faced Honeyeaters caught the eye. Closer attention was needed to identify the many smaller species among foliage and blossoms, Banded Honeyeaters, Rufous-throated Honeyeaters and Yellow-tinted Honeyeaters.

Not nectar-eaters, but winging their way through the woodlands, came spectacular Red-winged Parrots, and in pandanus palms below, parties of Crimson Finches.

This was tropical woodland at its peak, after the summer wet season, trees everywhere in full flower, grass still green, seeding, birds nesting everywhere.

Tropical woodlands and forests occur across northern Australia, from the Kimberleys in the west to north-eastern Queensland. The monsoon climate is the basis of this habitat, a climate of extremes. Tropical cyclonic storms, the torrential downpours of the summer wet season, flood the plains, send creeks in cascades and waterfalls down from the ranges. Moisture and heat produce explosive plant growth, when germinating grasses veil the dusty earth. Within a few months, in some places, the coarse grass can reach two, even three metres in height. The coming of the monsoon brings an equally great transformation for the wildlife, a burst of activity, and the water birds scatter wide across the newly rejuvenated wetlands.

In the tropical forests and woodlands the rain falls mostly from October to March; the winter dry season is almost totally rainless. High evaporation under the fierce tropical sun dries out the land far more rapidly than in southern regions, so that the extremely wet summer is swiftly followed by an equally dry time.

Eucalypt woodland and open forest is the most characteristic habitat across the north. Usually the dominant trees are the tall and graceful Stringybark and Darwin Woollybutt, the latter, *Eucalyptus miniata,* having white limbs and orange flowers. Along watercourses grow the tea-tree, *Melaleuca leucodendron,* reaching heights of around twenty metres. Their massive trunks have a papery bark, and from their branches grow a profusion of small white bottlebrush flowers which attract many birds.

The ground cover on the plains is principally of tall coarse grass, with scattered shrubs and smaller trees. Some have conspicuous flowers — Yellow-flowered Kapok Tree, the Cocky Apple, the unusual *Xanthostemon,* and a variety of wattles and grevilleas.

In more open woodlands, there are fewer of the tall Woollybutts and Stringybarks: Whitegums and Bloodwoods become more common. On sandstone ranges the woodland plant community includes, as well as the Darwin Woollybutt, *Eucalyptus miniata,* another orange-flowered, white-barked tree, *Eucalyptus phoeniceus;* the grass ground cover is replaced by a variety of small shrubs.

Tropical forests and woodlands can be seen in a number of national parks across northern Australia. In the Northern Territory, the Stuart Highway from Katherine to Darwin passes through these habitats. In Katherine Gorge grow woodlands of plains and of sandstone plateaux. Both of these also occur in Edith Falls National Park, a little further north.

Variety of flora and fauna, as well as beauty of scenery, are features of these parks. Within the overall tropical woodland habitat, they contain many variations, where gorges, rivers, rugged sandstone escarpments and flat plains all form part of the habitat.

In the Kimberleys, tropical woodlands and forests are an extremely widespread habitat. Roads from Derby and Fitzroy Crossing to Windjana and Geikie Gorge National Parks, pass through blacksoil plains woodlands, where large Baobab trees are a common feature.

Two large national parks in more remote areas of the Kimberleys, both preserving large areas of tropical woodland habitat are the Prince Regent River and Drysdale River National Parks.

The Prince Regent River area is mostly of extremely rugged sandstone country, deeply dissected by river gorges. Its extensive sandstone plateau has sparse open tropical woodland, with spinifex between large sandstone boulders. In valleys, the tall

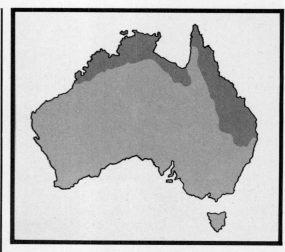

sorghum-type grass ground cover, beneath trees of *Eucalyptus latifolia, E. polycarpa* and *Grevillea pteridifolia.* Many variations of habitat occur, the species of woodland tree, and of the ground cover, varying in areas of lateritic plateau, basalt soil, and areas of alluvial creekside country. A survey of this reserve found 502 different plants, including 19 species of ferns, 43 lichens, 2 gymnosperms, and 419 flowering plants; however, this includes areas other than woodlands, such as small patches of semi-rainforest vine-thickets, and mangroves.

The Drysdale River National Park, also at present largely inaccessible by land, is mostly covered with low woodlands, of scattered eucalypts with an understorey of scattered shrubs and dense grasses.

Opposite page: The Edith River cascades down from the rugged western Arnhem Land escarpment in the Northern Territory. Edith Falls are not scenery on a grand scale, but have beauty in the exquisite natural detailing of the small cascades, clear pools and fringing tropical vegetation.

Right: Tumbling from the jagged sandstone escarpment of the north-western Kimberley region, the Mitchell Falls are an impressive sight even in the dry season. After the torrential rains of the tropical wet season the spectacle becomes awe-inspiring, but can be seen only from the air. Shown here is but one of an arc of falls, where the river divides and drops into two separate gorges. Surrounding Mitchell Falls, is a landscape of extremely rough sandstone ridges, of boulders and spinifex with scattered gums and intervening woodland flats. The wildlife of such a remote and inaccessible region remains plentiful, and in this locality includes Little Northern Native-cats, and the Water Pythons. Patches of semi-rainforest vegetation, known as monsoon forest or deciduous vine forest, grow in parts of the north-west Kimberley.

Above: One of Australia's largest frogs, with brilliant green, baggy-looking skin, and imposing visage is the Green Tree Frog *(Litoria caerulea).* Breeding populations gather in temporary wet season swamps. At other times they may be found in hollow limbs, and very often around or inside buildings, in cisterns, tanks, troughs or pipes. The Green Tree Frog occurs in regions of dominantly summer rainfall, from New South Wales through Queensland and tropical Northern Territory to the Kimberleys.

Right: The dragon lizard *Diporiphora bennetti* appears to have two separate populations. One is in the rugged Arnhem Land region of the Northern Territory, the other in rough ranges of the northern and eastern Kimberley. Minor differences are sufficient to allow these to be recognized as sub-species. If kept separated for sufficient time by climatic, landform or vegetation barriers, presumably they will continue to diverge until two full separate species exist. This dragon is a member of a genus of ten species, widely distributed from coastal Queensland into the south-west of the continent. Most species, however, are inhabitants of far northern Australia.

Right: Twenty-five species of bee-eaters occur throughout warm regions of the world, only one being present in Australia, the Rainbow Bee-eater. Bee-eaters hunt flying insects in open woodland country, or clearings of forests. They generally return to a favourite perch after each pursuit. There they beat the insect against the wood, very thoroughly in the case of bees, before eating them or taking them down to their nest. These birds come down to the ground only in the nesting season, for they are essentially creatures of the sky and treetops. When the young emerge from the nest tunnel they are plumaged like the adults. Until almost ready to fly, the young have their feathers wrapped in cylindrical waxy sheaths, which finally split off to reveal the bright plumage.

Left: Probably the most spectacular of Australian reptiles, the Frilled Lizard (*Chlamydosaurus kingii*) has developed to the full the survival tactics of surprise and bluff. The sudden impact of the display is all-important. At one moment the lizard is running, very fast, up on its hind legs, then suddenly it turns upon its foe, and explodes into a shape that, from the front, is instantly many times larger, with bright warning colours of red and orange around a gaping yellow mouth. For any predator that was about to seize a fleeing slender lizard this transformation must be alarming, if but for a few seconds. But this is all that the fleet-footed Frilled Lizard needs to reach the safety of a tree or spiny pandanus palm. The Frilled Lizard occurs across northern Australia from eastern coastal Queensland through the Northern Territory to the Kimberley region.

Left and below: Landing at its nest, a tunnel drilled into flat ground, a Rainbow Bee-eater displays the colourful plumage for which it was named. High-speed action photography reveals the great differences in wing and tail shapes between landing, and take-off. The bird descends with a fluttering, almost hovering action of wings, and with body held almost vertically. But often emerging from the nest tunnel, its take-off shows an entirely different action. The body is now horizontal, head up and aiming forward, wings reaching extremely wide and beating powerfully to thrust the bird almost explosively upwards, scattering grains of sand into the air. The ability to fly sets birds apart from most other vertebrates. Except for some of the largest birds, the action is too fast for the human eye to see, in detail, the plumage functioning in the manner for which it was evolved. Rainbow Bee-eaters *(Merops ornatus)* are summer visitors to southern parts of Australia, arriving in early September, and announcing their presence with shrill loud calls. During the summer these birds may be seen almost throughout Australia, except in heavily forested areas of the extreme south-east, south-west, and Tasmania.

Left: In the far northern tropical woodland belt the little Agile Wallaby is an extremely common animal. It inhabits tall grass country, with a preference for river floodplains, where the grass may be more palatable. It has a wide distribution across Australia from south-eastern Queensland around the eastern and northern coasts to the Kimberley region. The Agile Wallaby *(Macropus agilis)* was first seen by Europeans on the Coburg Peninsula, north-east of Darwin. The speed and agility with which these little wallabies eluded hunters and their dogs so impressed early naturalists that they gave the species the name *agilis.*

Right: At the extreme north-western tip of the Australian continent, between Admiralty Gulf and York Sound, the Mitchell Plateau is part of a wilderness of rough sandstone ranges. These render the deeply indented north-western coastline and its rugged hinterland one of the most inaccessible wilderness areas of Australia. The flat plateau-top is of hard laterite. The woodland of tropical palms under scattered tall eucalypts is unique. This canyon is known as Surveyor's Pool, where a creek has broken through the sandstone, and drops down a series of waterfalls. It is particularly beautiful when the last sunlight catches the cliffs which reflect in the darkly shadowed pools.

Left: Four of Australia's marsupial-mice are diminutive, some much smaller than an ordinary mouse, and are the smallest marsupials known to exist. Three of these have very flattened heads, and are called *Planigales,* the flat-skulled marsupial-mice. So small are they that when one attacks a large grasshopper, it becomes a battle between two creatures of almost equal size. These nervously active marsupials must consume a great amount of food, in proportion to their small size. The species shown here is the Pygmy Marsupial-mouse *(Antechinus maculatus)* which occurs in all mainland States, and is almost as small as the planigales.

Right: Huge, solid, beautifully silken-furred, a tropical spider pauses at the tower-like entrance of its burrow. Its hunting technique is to rush out when it detects by vibrations, that a beetle or other small prey is close by. The tips of this spider's front legs seem to have an iridescent red glow. The burrow was found on low-lying blacksoil plains country, which becomes waterlogged after heavy rain. The vertical extension of the burrow shape probably brings it above the usual water level, although the burrow is flooded up to the water level. The spider can wait just within this small mud tower, above water. Probably sensing by ground vibrations any approach, it cannot be surprised above the water, but will be found 30 or 40 cm underwater, at the bottom of the shaft. This spider is a form of, or close relative to, the Queensland spider *Seleno cosmia,* and must be regarded as dangerous.

Below: Hanging beneath the stalk of the tall, strong tropical woodland grass, a large female preying mantis carries the smaller males on her back. Their colour closely matches the dead grass of their environment. The mantis is one of the most deadly predators of the insect world, its long barbed forelimbs capable of rapid snatching strikes at any smaller insect venturing within range.

Above: The Red-backed Wren *(Malurus melanocephalus)* is quite distinctive in the 'fairy-wren' group, no other being red and black. These brilliant colours are worn only by the male during the breeding season. At other times both males and females are dull grey-brown above, whitish below. The preferred habitat is coarse grass, usually beneath scattered eucalypts of tropical woodland country. It occurs in regions of summer rainfall, north-eastern New South Wales, eastern and northern Queensland, and across northern Australia to the Kimberley region. The nest is a ball of grass with a side entrance, hidden in a small bush or grass tussock close to the ground.

Right: The Singing Honeyeater *(Meliphaga virescens)* ranges over a great variety of habitats, encompassing any area of trees or bushes except for rainforests. They are found in all States except Tasmania. This bird does not always live up to the name Singing Honeyeater, for many of its calls are harsh and unmusical. The 170 species of honeyeaters occuring in the south-west Pacific region typically have a slender down-curved bill, and a very long extensile brush-tipped tongue. The sides of the tongue curl inwards to form a tube through which nectar can be sucked. Very abundant among Australian birds, their success may be attributed to the abundance of flowering trees and other plants. The honeyeater family contains birds as diverse in appearance and size as, for example, the spinebill and the friar-birds. Australia has 70 species of which 54 are found only in Australia.

Left: In the King Leopold Ranges the tropical woodlands become more diverse and interesting than on the plains. There is variety of habitat, from rocky hills to permanently moist valleys with watercourses and gorges, all crowded into relatively small areas. Within a short distance can be found plants and animals of a wide range of habitat preferences. Yet the overall vegetation character remains one of open woodland. Trees are scattered widely, with occasional shrubs beneath, and grassy ground cover, or spinifex in the rocky places. On the plains around Darwin, the northern woodlands are dominated by the tall white-barked Darwin Woollybutt *(Eucalyptus miniata)*. In the hilly country of the Northern Territory this tree is replaced by a similar orange-flowered tree, *Eucalyptus phonenicea*. The Swamp Bloodwood occurs in the wet valleys. Thus the diverse habitats of the northern plains and ranges have a variety of attractive woodland trees, each with its own preference. Similarly, the wildlife indicates preferences, with this rough country containing such species as the White-quilled Rock-pigeon, the Black Grass-wren, and the Rock-haunting Ringtail Possum.

Above: The hibiscus group has many species in the far north and some extending into arid and southern regions. These shrubs, plus similar species of *Alyogyne, Gossypium* and others, are part of the tropical family Bombaceae, which also includes the Baobab bottle trees. The flora of tropical Australia is distinct from that of the south, for it is separated from the southern woodlands and forests by vast arid regions, and has much in common with islands to the north.

Above: Commonly known by the intriguing names of Cocky Apple and Billy-goat Plum, the tree *Planchonia careya* is widely distributed around northern Australia from tropical Queensland to the Northern Territory and the Kimberley region of Western Australia. The large flowers have delicate filamentous stamens which fall away easily. During the dry winter flowering, each flower lasts but a day, the mass of pink flowers soon carpeting the ground. The edible fruit is produced during the wet season.

Left: Confined to tropical forests and woodlands of northern Australia, the Banded Honeyeater *(Cissomela pectoralis)* is a neatly plumaged small bird of the treetops. Large numbers of these birds may be seen feeding at the flowers of such northern trees as this Darwin Woollybutt. Both male and female have, with small variations, a similar plumage pattern. In the crowns of the tall trees, these honeyeaters attract attention by their restless, active movements and tinkling calls. Their neat little nest is suspended by its rim in the foliage of a tree or shrub. In some localities, when trees are flowering, large numbers of these honeyeaters may be seen, being nomadic and wandering wherever nectar is abundant. The orange-flowered Darwin Woollybutt *(Eucalyptus miniata)* is a common tree in the woodlands of the Northern Territory and Kimberley region of Western Australia.

Right: Found only in far northern Australia, the Yellow-tinted Honeyeater *(Meliphaga flavescens)* is a bird of the riverside trees and thickets, and adjacent tropical woodlands. Its range of distribution extends from northern Queensland through the Northern Territory to the western Kimberley region. Often small flocks of 20 or 30 birds will be seen working through the foliage seeking nectar and insects. These birds closely resemble in appearance and behaviour the White-plumed Honeyeaters which inhabit regions further south; the White-plumed has, however, a white instead of black ear streak or plume. Wildflowers provide honeyeating birds directly with only part of their food, the nectar. But indirectly the flowers provide other nourishment, their nectar attracting insects. These in turn bring spiders and other predatory insects, making the flowers rich hunting grounds for birds.

Left: The Brindled Bandicoot *(Isoodon macrourus)* inhabits the undergrowth of thickets in woodlands and forests of north-eastern New South Wales, eastern Queensland, and tropical northern Australia. Its fur is of a golden brown, finely speckled black, giving a brindled appearance. The fur of bandicoots is rather harsh, made up of long outer guard hairs beneath which is softer under-fur. Brindled Bandicoots from the Northern Territory and Kimberley are of the lighter, more golden coloration shown. The Brindled Bandicoot is one of the short-nosed bandicoots group, of which Australia has three species. Although it appears to have a long nose, this is not long when compared with that of the real long-nosed bandicoots, of which the Little Marl is one example. The Bandicoots in general seem quite tolerant of human interference. The Brindled Bandicoot is still common near Darwin, the Common Hairy-nosed Bandicoot is abundant around Sydney, and the Southern Short-nosed Bandicoot in the hill suburbs of Perth.

Left: In wet soils by watercourses, freshwater swamps and springs of the tropical woodlands of the 'top end' of the Northern Territory, the Swamp Bloodwood, *Eucalyptus ptychocarpa*, often grows to a large size. The bloodwood group of eucalypts is so named for the red kino that exudes from crevices of the bark. The large heads of flowers are carried at the ends of the branches, and create a conspicuous display, white on some trees, but usually bright red. A most attractive feature is the foliage, of exceptionally large leaves, up to 30 cm long, and 10 cm wide. There are in tropical northern Australia four trees with reddish flowers. Two are of orange-red colour, and with smooth white upper trunk and limbs, while this species and one other have flowers of white through pink to red, and rough fibrous bark. One other species is the Rough-leaved Bloodwood *(Eucalyptus setosa)*.

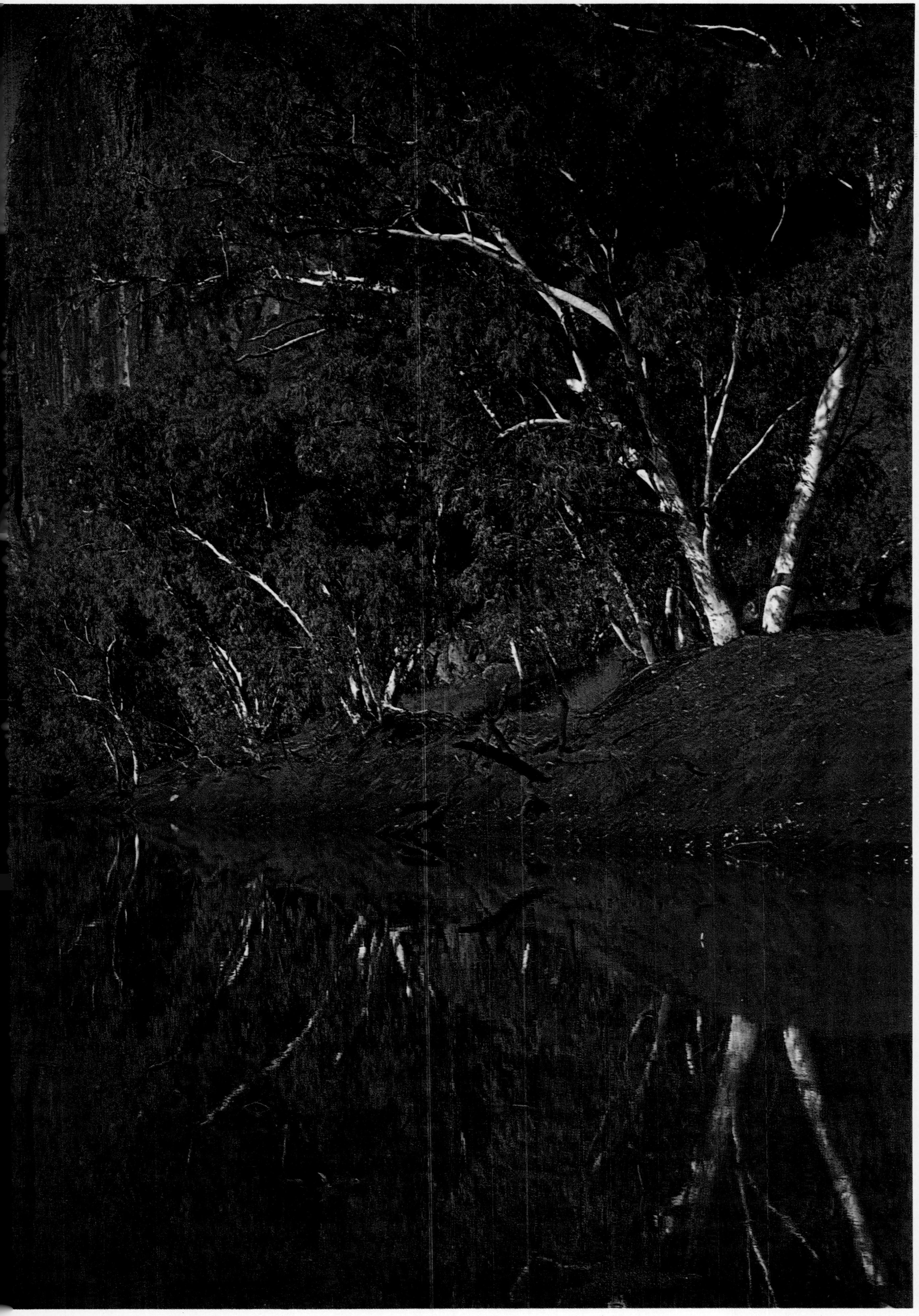

Previous page: In both northern Queensland and the far north of Western Australia, ancient limestone ranges rise above the tropical woodland plains like huge grey stone castle walls and towers. These were formed beneath the sea as coral barrier reefs. The Queensland examples are at Chillago, west of Cairns, and beneath these are well-known tourist caves. In the Kimberley region, the ancient reefs are remarkably well preserved. Through these, the Napier and Oscar Ranges, several rivers have cut spectacular gaps and gorges, the most famous being Geikie Gorge and Wandjana Gorge. Their permanent pools are used by the birds and wallabies of the surrounding woodlands, and have their own inhabitants such as Fresh-water Crocodiles, and Flying Foxes.

Left and above: The large bulging eyes of the Brown Tree Snake (*Boiga irregularis*) are indicative of its nocturnal habits. By day, rock crevices, caves, hollow trees, or the spiny centres of a pandanus palm are favourite hiding places. It emerges at night to hunt for birds, small mammals and lizards. The long, slender lithe body makes it fast among the branches and foliage of trees. The wide head and narrow neck of this snake give the impression that it is a python, but it is actually one of the venomous snakes. Australia has very few snakes of the Colubrid family, the snake family dominant elsewhere in the world. The Brown Tree Snake differs from most other Australian venomous snakes in having its fangs at the rear of its mouth rather than at the front, and is not venomous to man.

Left: The world's largest snakes are the pythons and boas, a family of bulky non-venomous constrictors. The prey is killed by the python coiling around and tightening until it is suffocated. Like most other snakes, the pythons are able to swallow prey much larger than the diameter of their own bodies by expansion outwards and their loosely connected jaws. Australia has about ten python species, of which the largest is the Amethystine, which can exceed 8 m in length. The python shown here sunning itself on a flat rock beside a river pool is the Water Python (*Liasis mackloti*) which grows to a length of about 3 m.

Right: This quite attractive-looking native rat inhabits a wide variety of country including savannah woodlands, coastal flats and river floodplains. It occurs in northern Australia, from Queensland and New South Wales through the Northern Territory to the north-west coast. Known both by the names Paler Field-rat and Tunney's Rat *(Rattus tunnei)* this species has a short tail, and long fine soft fur usually giving a rather fluffy appearance, except when it has been running through wet vegetation. Like other bush rats, the species still bears the generic name *Rattus,* indicating that it is not greatly different from the rats of other continents. But being entirely a bush creature, it is comparatively clean. The length of time that the bush rats have been isolated in Australia is perhaps in the order of tens of thousands of years, not sufficient for great evolutionary changes.

Right: The Bar-breasted Honeyeater builds a nest that is most unusual among Australian honeyeaters. It is one of only two species which build domed nests, the other being the Brown-backed Honeyeater of coastal north-eastern Queensland. The nest is very large for so small a bird. The entrance is an opening on one side. The preferred site is near the tip of a branch overhanging water, either a stream or a paperbark swamp. Although not usually very high, the nests can be difficult to reach except from the water. The Bar-breasted Honeyeater *(Ramsayornis fasciatus)* has been recorded nesting at various times of the year, winter, spring, summer and autumn, and probably nests whenever conditions are favourable. These birds are nomadic, following the flowering of tropical trees, finding both insects and nectar. They occur across northern Australia from Rockhampton to Broome.

DESERTS AND ARID STEPPE-LANDS

The scene which most closely conforms to the desert image is one of an almost endless expanse of bare, barren dunes and rock, a lifeless wasteland over which reigns a pitiless fiery sun. But although Australia's deserts are of enormous extent, nowhere are they totally barren, and most parts are only moderately arid compared with the deserts of some other continents.

In its mood of drought, the desert's sparse vegetation reveals the true face of the land. This is a world of eroded ranges, rippled dunes, stone-paved plains, glaring white salt lakes. But even through the most prolonged droughts the tough desert vegetation of the mulga scrub, saltbush and spinifex, manages to survive.

The drought is broken briefly by the coming of rain. With the life-giving touch of moisture, a fresh green mantle of new growth spreads across and begins to conceal the earth, fast covering the bare space. Perennial plants, responding to the water reaching down to their roots, put out fresh green shoots. Spinifex, that tough needle-pointed drought-survivor, changes from sun-bleached straw colour to deep green.

The greatest transformation comes from the ephemeral plants, the short-lived, soft-stemmed everlastings, mulla-mullas, succulents and grasses. They have but a few weeks for growth, flowering and setting of seed. These plants are not adapted to survive when the drought returns, but their seeds are, and spring to life to renew the species whenever rain again penetrates the desert.

With the coming of rain to the desert there is also a rebirth of animal life, ranging from tiny shield shrimps and frogs which appear in the muddy claypans, to the desert birds which, in a burst of conspicuous activity and song, nest and rear their young while the desert is so briefly generous.

Australia's desert regions contain a diversity of vegetation types. Very few areas conform to the desert stereotype of a lifeless region. Scenically, the geology dominates the sparse vegetation. There are jagged ranges of colourful rock, and awe-inspiring gorges, vast plains of gibber-stones glittering like mosaics of mirrors. Unending variety is to be seen in breakaway-edged mesas, dry sandplains, treeless shrub plains, rippled ridges of dunes, and scrubby mulga flats.

In contrast, where there is permanent water, as in the depths of gorges, there are scenes of lush-foliaged River Red Gums, Cadjeputs and palms. Where moisture seeps from shadowed cliff walls there are delicate ferns and mosses.

The vast desert and semi-desert heartland touches upon all mainland States, comprising large parts of the interior of South Australia, the Northern Territory, Queensland, New South Wales and Western Australia. Most of the semi-desert edges of large parts of Central Australia are quite well vegetated, carrying mulga or mallee scrub, or spinifex vegetation, as described elsewhere in this book. These habitats extend into the most arid parts, becoming more sparse, more subject to drought, and are then more appropriately described as desert.

Australia's most notorious desert regions are well known by name. Closest to the south-eastern centres of population is the Simpson Desert. But covering immense areas further west and north-west are the Tanami Desert, the Great Sandy Desert, Gibson Desert and the Great Victoria Desert. All, in fact, merge imperceptibly with each other and with the surrounding semi-desert fringes, so that their precise boundaries are of no real significance.

The Simpson Desert covers a vast tract about the junction of the borders of Queensland, New South Wales and South Australia. This is a region of consolidated parallel sand dunes running in a north-south direction determined by the prevailing wind direction.

Probably Australia's most famous of desert tracks are those that cross arid country at the eastern edge of the Simpson from South Australia into Queensland and north-western New South Wales. These are the Birdsville Track from Marree to Birdsville, and the Strzelecki Track from the northern Flinders Ranges to Innamincka and thence into New South Wales.

The Birdsville Track follows flats of lake country and watercourses, the overflow country of the Diamantina River, and the normally dry Goyder Lagoon, avoiding most of the dunes. Here on the flats of the channel country and around Lake Eyre are extensive areas of low Saltbush and Bluebush, making a shrub steppe habitat. The track also crosses gibber-stone country where highly polished quartz stones form a gleaming mosaic pavement across the plains.

The western desert region of the Northern Territory is one of the most remote regions in Australia, bordering on the Great Sandy Desert. But this

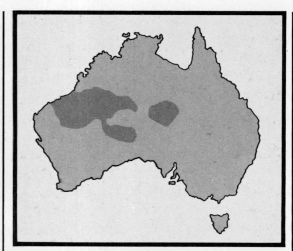

region is becoming increasingly attractive to visitors to Central Australia, with improved access in recent years. Roads now lead beyond the western MacDonnell Ranges. Further south, the multitude of visitors to Ayers Rock and Mt. Olga are at the edge of the western deserts. Now it is possible to continue by road further west, past the Olgas, into the spectacular desert ranges around the junction of the borders of Western Australia, the Northern Territory and South Australia.

This track, which should never be attempted in summer months or without the necessary permit to pass through Aboriginal reserves, passes into Western Australia via the Docker River settlement, Giles Meteorological Station, the Warburton Mission, Laverton and Leonora, eventually to Kalgoorlie.

Opposite page: Large areas of Australian desert plains are stony, sometimes almost completely hiding the earth beneath. The effect varies, the landscape sometimes being covered with white quartz, elsewhere with black rocks so polished by wind-blown sand that they gleam in the bright sunlight.

Right: Like a miniature, mouse-sized kangaroo, the Wuhl-wuhl or Jerboa-marsupial has long hind legs and tail, but here the kangaroo resemblance ends. At speed it does not bound along on hind legs, but touches with both fore-feet and hind. The very long, brush-tipped tail seems to act as a rudder, enabling the speeding animal to make abrupt changes in direction almost in mid-leap. The Wuhl-wuhl (*Antechinomys spenceri*) is an insect hunter of the dry inland, and although superficially like the rodent-hopping mice of those regions, is not a rodent but a marsupial carnivore. This delightful creature inhabits arid regions from western Queensland to the interior of Western Australia.

Left: Maps of Australia show great numbers of lakes scattered across even the most arid central regions. The largest and most famous is the 'inland sea' of Lake Eyre, but others of great size include Lake Amadeus, Lake Mackay, Lake Carnegie and Lake Disappointment. Almost always these are dry, their surfaces a clay crust, white with salt. After rare flooding, rains may fill and link them together, re-creating ancient river patterns of a past wetter climate. Most rains do no more than dampen the salt and clay, or at best cover the flat lake beds with a water depth of a few centimetres, or very rarely a metre or two. Lake Alba, beside the Canning Stock Route through the Gibson Desert, is surrounded by red desert dunes where only low mulga scrub and spinifex grow. At times this landscape possesses a certain harsh beauty, as in late afternoon, when the low sun casts shadows across the rippled sand.

Right: The light-green-foliaged, prostrate stems of the Sturt Desert Pea radiate outwards, and interlock with surrounding plants. The red desert soil damp from the rain which germinated the seeds, is visible only through gaps in the spreading cover of the plants. The flowers are always spectacular, held above the foliage, and are most striking when seen *en masse* against the sun, when their translucent red colour seems afire against shadowy backlit surroundings. White-flowered plants occur occasionally among the red, and some have a maroon rather than black centre. The Sturt Pea (*Clianthus formosus*) is found throughout the drier areas of Australia.

Left: Across mulga scrublands and arid woodlands of inland Australia the calls of the Spiny-cheeked Honeyeater *(Acanthagenys rufogularis)* are a part of the character of this harsh yet beautiful environment. When it is seen, the bright pink bill is conspicuous, as are the white, spiny-looking cheek patches. These honeyeaters are often encountered in small flocks where trees or shrubs are flowering. As well as nectar, this species seeks native berries including those of mistletoe, and takes large numbers of insects. The nest is a delight of efficient construction, a small light basket of grasses bound with spiders webs, and delicately suspended by its rim from a slender branch in the outer foliage of a tree or large shrub. The Spiny-cheeked Honeyeater occurs through inland regions of all States except Tasmania.

Left: Scattered and stunted eucalypts occur through many of Australia's remote deserts, usually too few and too small to make a woodland formation. One of Australia's most spectacular flowering eucalypts is native to some of the most wild remote country, the desert to the west and to the south-east of the junction of the borders of South Australia, the Northern Territory and Western Australia. Although called the Large-fruited Mallee, the usual form of growth of this species, *Eucalyptus youngiania,* is of a single-trunked tree up to 10 m in height. Not only are individual flowers among the largest of the eucalypts, but they occur in groups of three, often aggregated into as many as fifteen larger clusters, forming a fiery sphere some 25 cm in diameter. The buds, which take almost a year to form, are large, intense green and deeply ribbed.

Above: Active, alert, with long bushy tail bristling, a hunting Kowari moves in quick jerky stop-start movements, occasionally standing on hind legs to look around. This marsupial carnivore could be described as the native cat of the deserts. Although smaller, it has the same fearless, tenacious, restlessly active temperament. By night it hunts for insects, ground-nesting birds, lizards, and probably small mammals such as hopping mice and marsupial mice. After sunrise it retires to a burrow, the usual daytime refuge. The Kowari *(Dasyuroides byrnei)* is confined to central Australia, in a region near the Simpson Desert, around the junction of the borders of Queensland, the Northern Territory and South Australia. Although a marsupial, the pouch is but slightly developed, with side folds of skin enclosing the mammary area.

Right: If good rains have fallen on desert plains during early spring months, the red clay will be almost concealed by the massed gold of the papery everlastings. A few months later, only their remnants will remain. These flowers are of the species *Cephilipterum drummondii,* of the large family Compositae. Each flower consists of a large compound head of many tiny flowers crowded together.

Left: Beautifully marked to blend with the golds, reds and browns of spinifex, red sand and rock, the Desert Death-adder *(Acanthophis pyrrhus)* is widespread, but not often seen when lying motionless in wait for its prey. This is one of Australia's most venomous and dangerous snakes, although it rarely attains a length of more than 75 cm. Its body is broad and flat, with a wide triangular head that is very distinctly separated from the body by a narrow neck. The short thick body terminates in a thin little tail, which has a whitish spine-like tip. This peculiar tail appears to function as a lure. The Death-adder lies in a coiled, ready-to-strike position, with the tail brought around in line with its head. If a lizard or other small creature approaches the tail tip, it is wriggled. Any lizard that rushes in to capture what appears to be food, becomes, in one lightning-fast strike, the prey of the snake. The Desert Death-adder is found through central Australia, from far western Queensland to north-western Australia. A similar, but less colourful species, the Common Death-adder, inhabits coastal regions.

Previous page: Through the desert ranges rivers have carved valleys and gorges, probably in past ages with a much wetter climate. Steep river gorges are a prominent feature of Australia's deserts, and many of these present a spectacular display of bold colours. Rock and raw earth colours are exposed, only very slightly concealed by vegetation. Beside the pools, River Gums provide cool shade, while the gum tree foliage is a refreshing colour contrast. Some of the most impressive gorges are in Australia's north-west; Red Gorge, one of the major canyons of the Hamersley Ranges, is very long, and becomes deeper and narrower further upstream. Roads lead into the lower gorge. The narrow parts deep in the range have access roads along the range top, where the best view is from a lookout at the junction of Red Gorge, Weino Gorge and Hancock Gorge.

Left: The knob-tailed Gecko *Nephrurus laevissimus* inhabits desert country of the Northern Territory, South Australia and Western Australia. It appears to prefer spinifex-covered sand dune and sandplain country. Six species of knob-tailed geckos are similar in overall big-headed, stumpy, knob-tailed appearance, but with individual identifying details. The largest grows to about 100 mm length; the species pictured reaches about 80 mm. All are inhabitants of desert or semi-arid country although one, *Nephrurus asper,* occurs also in rocky areas of tropical woodland country of northern Australia. Being inhabitants of such remote regions, few have common names.

Above: Commonly known as the Broad-banded Sand-swimmer, this small skink is found almost throughout inland regions of Australia, from the Great Dividing Range to the western coast. Its name presumably derives from its wriggling swimming action in soft sand, where the tiny limbs have little effect. This species was formerly known as *Sphenomorphus richardsonii,* but now as *Eremiascincus richardsonii.* Small skinks are most often seen sunbasking, or are found hiding under bush debris.

Right: One of the best-known of Australian birds throughout the world must be the Budgerigar. But in aviaries these birds, no matter what their colour, cannot equal the spectacle presented by the huge flocks of thousands of birds, brilliant green in the intense sunlight, seen against red rock gorge walls, or golden spinifex. After rain the flocks of Budgerigars break up, and pairs select nest holes in the gums that line most inland watercourses, or in small hollows of stunted mulga trees. While the female is incubating the male arrives at regular intervals to feed her at the nest entrance with the grass seeds he has collected. Budgerigars, like many arid country birds, react quickly to breed almost immediately after rain, and in a good season may rear several broods in quick succession. They inhabit arid spinifex, mulga and saltbush plains, and arid woodlands throughout the continent, except for forested coastal regions.

Left: The River Gums of Ormiston Gorge give cool shade with their abundant bright green foliage. These trees in moist situations even in central Australia reach massive size, and with age develop hollows that provide nesting places for birds. Those that grow where floodwaters sweep down the gorge are often broken, but shoot up again. As well as the hollows, the height of the trees attracts eagles, hawks, harrier and crows. For travellers in often hot and dusty regions, the river gorges are welcome stopping places. Clear pools mirror the white-trunked gums and red cliffs, making places of refreshing beauty.

Right: The Orange Chat *(Ephthianura aurifrons)* is a bird of the most arid central Australian regions, where it prefers the low samphire and saltbush vegetation around the margins of claypans and saltlakes. This species, in common with many birds of very open habitats, tends to be wary and difficult to approach. Its secretive tactics make the well hidden nest, although close to the ground, quite difficult to find. Orange Chats are highly nomadic, wandering in large parties away from drought-stricken regions to areas experiencing more favourable conditions. They may be found in dry regions of western New South Wales, western Queensland, south-western Victoria, South Australia, the Northern Territory and Western Australia.

Right: As the claypan mud dries out, cracks appear, creating a jigsaw of irregular interlocking shapes. Where the surface sediments are extremely fine, the surface even when dry remains glossy, as if varnished. This accentuates the colours of the clay, the rusty reds, sienna and burnt umber tones, equalling the glaze and depths of colour of fired pottery. If the slabs are very thin, they will curl into cylindrical shapes, giving the drying claypan areas of rough texture as well as of gloss and colour. The beauty of the desert claypans is short-lived. Wind soon destroys its most fragile creations, and dust soon fills and obscures the patterns of cracks, the colours and gloss, leaving the lakebed or claypan an uninteresting flat red-dust wasteland until the coming of the next heavy rains.

Left: The gibber-stone plains are mantled with polished stones which range in size from large boulders to tiny pebbles. Most have been smoothed and polished by wind-blown sand until they resemble glossy gemstones. They may be of translucent white quartz with angular flat surfaces that glimmer under the intense sunlight, or jet black but so highly polished that, seen against the light, they sparkle across the plains like the pathway of moonlight over rippled water. Individual stones may have markings, specks or lines of gemstone colours. The most famed of such desert surfaces, recorded in early explorations east of Lake Eyre, is Sturt's Stony Desert. The gibber-stone plains are remarkable phenomena, as many of the stones actually work their way up through the clay to the surface. The alternating, seasonal wetting and drying of the clay, over thousands of years, has moved the rocks upwards.

Left: On pavement-hard flats, rain quickly forms broad shallow pools and lakes. Even if covering many hectares in area, most usually have but a few centimetres depth. Although the rain and the flooding may bring a rush of animal life, with Avocets and Stilts nesting on small islands of the lakes, and Orange Chats in the low samphire scrub of the lake or claypan shores, the water remains only a very few months. As the water level drops the flat muddy claypan lake bottom is exposed. At first a slithery soupy thin mud, it soon firms as water is sucked up by the scorching desert sun. While the surface is still soft, the footprints of desert animals, Emus, Red Kangaroos, and wading birds, are in many places recorded in the mud. The clay settles from the muddy water in layers, the coarsest sediments falling quickly to the bottom, the finest colloidal clays remaining suspended until last. When the claypan surface is exposed by the receding water, it is in layers. As it breaks into tile-like slabs, the different amount of shrinkage between fine top layers and coarse bottom layers causes each piece to curve or curl.

Right: Across each desert dune the winds sculpt rippled patterns of smooth symmetry. Over this texture the sunlight glances low, morning and evening, catching the tops of the ripples. Highlights and shadows define patterns which are scarcely visible for most of the day under overhead sun. The sand is a surface upon which the desert's living creatures record their presence. Small footprints record the presence of small mammals, the Kowari, Mulgara or Wuhl-wuhl, larger imprints reveal the stealthy stalking of Dingo or feral cat, or the passing of a camel. An undulating line may have been left by a small snake, long ridges show that a beetle, burrowing lizard or snake, has ploughed a tunnel just beneath the surface. Tiny dimpled markings reveal the wanderings of beetles and centipedes. This record of sand-dune life is brief, soon erased by the rising wind.

Above: The Emu stands almost 2 m tall, and although flightless is capable of running at speeds up to 50 km per hour. It seems not greatly slowed by spinifex clumps, scrub or rocks, the great strides of the armour-plated feet and legs carrying it over most obstacles with scarcely a falter in stride. The small head is thrust out in front finding gaps in scrub through which the big body follows, pounding along behind, thorny branches glancing off the thick covering of coarse feathers.

The Emu (Dromarius novaehollandiae) was once found throughout Australia except for north-eastern rainforests. Although gone from the more closely settled localities, it still inhabits large parts of the continent, remaining abundant in many remote semi-desert regions. At times of drought Emus will move and, on such occasions, sometimes form huge flocks, that may invade outlying farms and cause considerable damage. The Emu is an autumn-nesting bird. Six to eleven very large grey-green eggs are laid on the ground, and are immediately deserted by the female. Incubation is the duty of the male, who must care for the striped chicks for as long as 18 months.

Right: Where a tributary of the Finke River has cut through the MacDonnell Ranges at the foot of Mt. Sonder, the exposed rock of Ormiston Gorge is among the most colourful in this part of the Northern Territory. Cliffs of dark red, rust and white rock frame a view through to distant blue ranges. The vegetation of the ranges is of small shrubs and tough small trees, with spinifex as the dominant ground cover. In some parts of the MacDonnells, rock wallabies still occur, secure in the rough ranges.

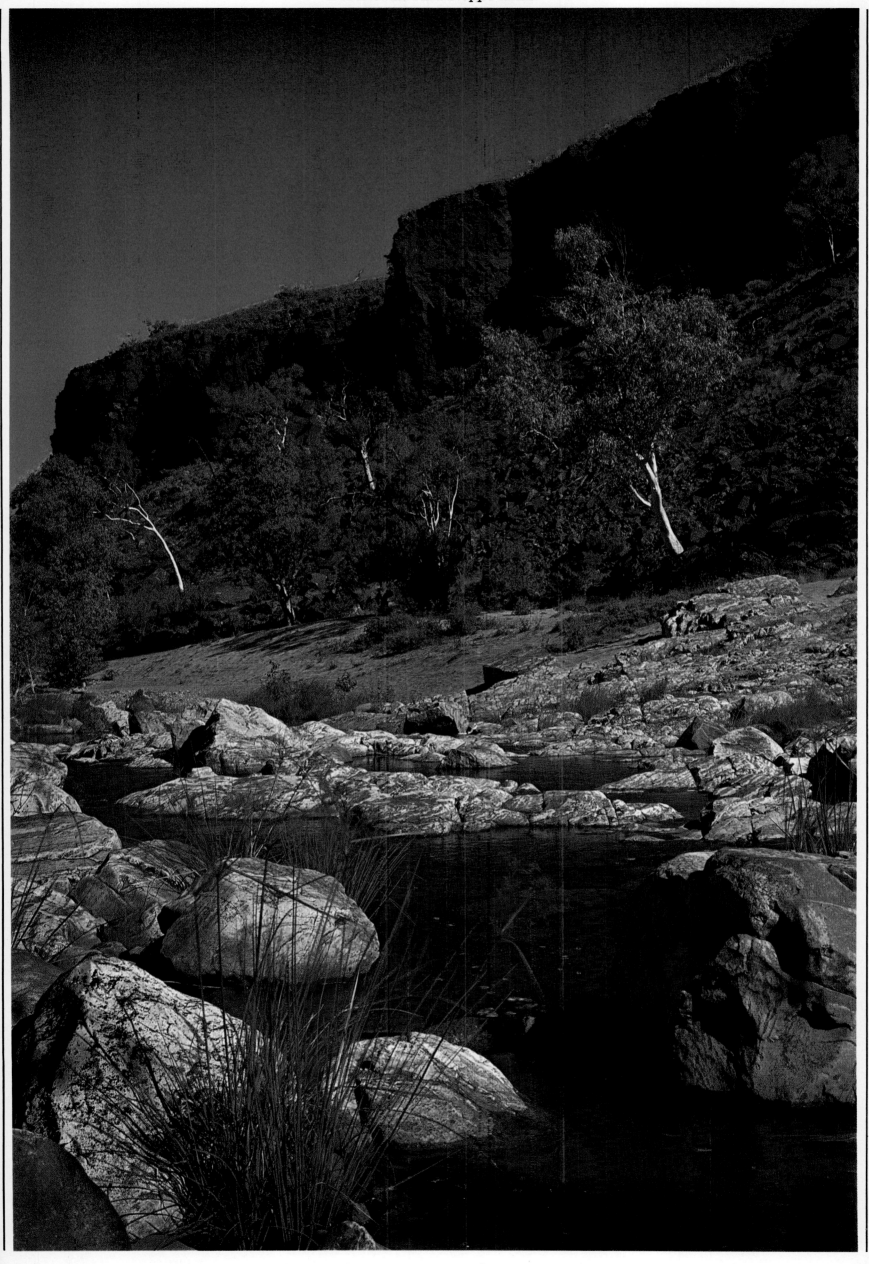

TEMPERATE AND ALPINE WOODLANDS

With rust-red striped back arched and bristling tail held vertically, a Numbat sends sticks and dirt flying with rapid impatient jerks of its paws, rasping with its claws into the flimsy termite-riddled wood of a half-buried log. It pauses, paw frozen in mid-air, alert and listening for danger, then begins to feed, its long tongue flickering into the hollowed termite galleries. This is a scene in Wandoo woodland country, the habitat of one of Australia's most beautifully coloured marsupials, the Numbat or Banded Anteater.

Like most other small marsupials, this creature has little chance of defending itself against the larger predators, eagles, dingoes, foxes, cats, or large pythons. Speed is its only chance. At the first sight or sound of danger, rustle of leaves or snapping of twigs, generally it dashes away immediately through the bushes, headed for one of the secure refuges within its familiar home territory. Its sanctuaries at time of danger are hollow logs — the fallen hollow limbs or trunks of one of the woodland trees.

To burn or otherwise remove these logs, which superficially appear to be of no value except perhaps as firewood, is to leave the Numbat totally vulnerable, with little chance of survival. Every bush creature is dependent upon the preservation of its natural bush habitat; for another animal it might not be the logs, but instead, a certain kind of dense undergrowth, or long grass, or thickets of young trees.

The Wandoo woodlands are just one example of a habitat very widespread in southern parts of Australia. In woodlands the trees are more widely spaced than in forests, with rounded crowns that do not interlock overhead. Most woodlands occur between the coastal forests and the drier mallee or mulga scrubs of the interior, and altogether cover a far greater portion of the continent than do the forests.

Beneath their open canopy there is a ground cover which in some regions is of grasses, and elsewhere of low scrub undergrowth, forming either savannah-woodlands or shrub-woodlands. The woodlands of eastern Australia tend often to have grass ground covers, those of south-western Australia an undergrowth of a variety of flowering shrubs.

The woodland habitat is so extensive and so varied in composition that space does not permit even a brief

description of more than a very few examples.

In eastern Australia, temperate woodlands occur mainly to the east of the Great Dividing Range, from south-eastern Queensland through New South Wales to south-western Victoria, and in eastern Tasmania. The Divide is a major watershed. On its eastern slopes the heavier rainfall supports forests; to the west, the drier inland slopes are mostly clothed in open woodlands.

Parts of the Divide have areas of alpine woodland. The New England Tableland at altitudes around 900 to 1200 metres where winter snowfalls are common, has woodlands of Snow Gums. On lower parts of the tableland the savannah-woodlands form a rather open landscape, where a common tree is the New England Peppermint, with rough brown bark and gnarled trunk.

Woodlands occur further south, on the inland slopes of the Great Divide, west of the Blue Mountains, where typical trees are the Yellow Box, the Grey Box and the Bimble Box. The Warrumbungles National Park preserves woodlands of Yellow Bloodwood, Cypress Pine and Scribbly Gums on the poorer soils, and elsewhere, woodlands of White Box.

Kosciusko National Park contains a great diversity of natural vegetation, including temperate woodlands. Woodlands of several box species of eucalypt grow on areas of good soils along the lower Snowy River. In the higher colder woodlands the eucalypts are the Manna Gum, the Broad-leaved Sally and the Black Sally. Near the winter snow line, the trees become dwarfed by the rigorous conditions, forming sub-alpine woodlands of Snow Gums, continuing up to an altitude of about 2000 metres.

Temperate woodlands are a feature of the vegetation of the Australian Capital Territory, where the major reserve is Tidbinbilla. Savannah-woodlands cover much of the plains, with low eucalypts and Wallaby Grass beneath. The commonest of the woodland trees on the lowlands are the Yellow Box, the Red Box, Blakely's Red Gum and the Apple Box. In most places the original woodlands have been modified for farming activities. The high mountain ridges have several species of Snow Gum, forming sub-alpine woodlands. During the summer months the ground beneath the Snow Gums is carpeted with many flowers, such as the Yellow Billy Buttons. Flowering shrubs here are the Bitter

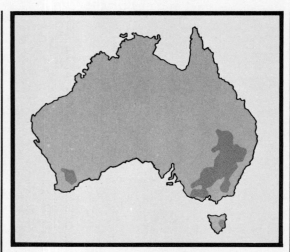

Pea, and several orange and red-flowered species of Oxylobium.

The high woodlands have many herbaceous plants which appear and flower after the melting of the snowfields in summer, including Golden Everlastings, Golden Lilies, Bluebells, Snow Daisies, Billy Buttons and Eyebrights. Grass Trigger-plants in some areas carpet the ground beneath the Snow Gums.

On the opposite side of the continent, in the woodland region of the southern interior of Western Australia, the Lake Magenta Fauna Reserve preserves a large sample of temperate woodland habitat. Here the trees are Salmon Gums, smaller Swamp Mallets, White Mallets, and Stocking Trees. The graceful Salmon Gum is a remarkable woodland species in that it reaches a height of 25 to 30 metres on a rainfall as low as 250 millimetres.

Opposite page: The trees of the temperate woodlands are in many districts slender and graceful, with umbrella-shaped crowns below which there is little foliage. So distinctive is their silhouette that it is immediately recognizable as eucalypt woodlands.

Right: The Yellow Robin, which inhabits forests and woodlands of Australia's eastern coast, once extended along the south coast to Western Australia. An increasingly arid climate made large sections of the habitat unsuitable, leaving isolated populations in the south-west corner of the continent, and on Eyre Peninsula, South Australia. These isolated populations have gradually changed, presumably a result of an environmental difference. Where the Eastern Yellow Robin has bright yellow on both breast and abdomen, the western birds have acquired, over thousands of years, a grey area above the yellow. The Western Yellow Robin *(Eopsaltria griseogularis)* has thus evolved as a separate species. Here, one of these birds visits its neat nest, which is camouflaged by strips of bark.

Left: The tall shrub sometimes called Red Pokers is equally well known by its scientific name of *Hakea bucculenta*. Red Pokers grows in an environment of tall shrubs and banksia trees, with scattered patches of eucalypts, forming a banksia-eucalypt woodland and heathlands complex. This varies in composition within its range of distribution, near Australia's mid-western coast, extending from temperate into semi-arid areas. Spectacular both at a distance, and close-up, this shrub has long flower spikes that are not concealed by the fine foliage. In its natural habitat it is much frequented by birds, which in that region include the Spiny-cheeked Honeyeater, Tawny-crowned Honeyeater, Singing Honeyeater and Brown Honeyeater.

Left: The tree, Illyarrie, creates a colourful late summer display. This is native to banksia-eucalypt woodlands of the sandplain coastal strip of Australia's western coastline, in the vicinity of the Irwin River and the Moore River. For several months before flowering, the intricately sculptured buds are very ornamental, deep green with bright red caps. As the tree, *Eucalyptus erythrocorys,* bursts into flower the red caps fall away to allow the deep yellow filaments to unfold. For approximately a month, the tree is a spectacle of both red and yellow but gradually changes from a red to a yellow display. The tree as a whole is white-trunked, and attractive even when not in flower.

The Sacred Kingfisher commonly chooses a hollow of a tree as its nest site, or drills a tunnel into a termite nest in a tree. As this bird flies in and out of the nest entrance it shows the wing positions associated with this action. The Sacred Kingfisher *(Halcyon sancta)* is one of the better-known Australian kingfishers, being found throughout the continent except for arid central regions. It occurs in a wide variety of habitats, including woodlands, forests, along rivers of inland regions, and in coastal mangrove swamps. Only occasionally does this species hunt for fish, or other aquatic prey; usually it feeds upon dry-land creatures, such as small lizards, spiders and grasshoppers.

Sacred Kingfishers defend their nests with great vigour. They will dive with a loud screech upon any intruder near the nest, coming very close with the large sharp bill, and at a velocity likely to do damage if impact occurs. An indication of the solid structure of bill, head and neck of these birds is shown by their nest-digging technique. When beginning to drill into a termite nest, the birds fly at the hard material, striking it beak-first, each time chipping out a small piece. The kingfisher family is divided into two main groups, the wood-kingfishers and the true kingfishers. The wood-kingfishers do not usually hunt fish, but prey upon small land animals, especially frogs, small reptiles and insects. Australian wood-kingfishers

include the two species of kookaburras, the Red-backed Kingfisher, the Forest Kingfisher, Yellow-billed, White-tailed, Mangrove and Sacred Kingfishers. The true kingfishers are the fish-hunters, which plunge into water to take their prey. There are only two Australian true kingfishers, the Azure Kingfisher and the Little Kingfisher.

The Sacred Kingfisher is a migratory species. Although quite common in most of Australia, they inhabit southern parts only during the summer months. For the winter months these birds retreat to tropical northern Australia, with some individuals travelling to Timor, Sumatra and other Indonesian islands.

Each year the Sacred Kingfishers arrive in the southern States regularly in the first half of September. They announce their presence with loud calls, 'ki-ki-ki-ki'. Nesting is from October to January; around March the kingfishers leave again for the far north.

This kingfisher's nest is a tunnel and chamber drilled into an arboreal termite nest, a terrestrial termite mound, or into a creek bank. At other times natural hollows of trees are chosen. In Western Australia hollows in trees are invariably used, at any height up to 20 m above the ground. No nest is constructed; five white eggs are simply laid on the bare soil or wood dust.

Right: The Numbat or Marsupial Anteater *(Myrmecobius fasciatus)* is becoming one of Australia's rare mammals, and one of the most specialized. One of the marsupial carnivores, it has for so long concentrated exclusively upon termites as its only food, it now shows considerable adaptations. The Numbat's face has become very slender-pointed, and the long thin tongue can be extended as much as 10 cm, so that it can lick termites from the nest tunnels. Small, soft-bodied white ants require no tearing apart, so the Numbat's teeth have become extremely small. The Numbat survives now in two regions. One is the Everard Ranges in the far north-west of South Australia. Recently in the second, the Wandoo woodlands and forests of the south-west of Western Australia, there appears to have been a serious fall in its numbers.

Left: At night, almost anywhere in the Australian bush, will be heard the pleasant double-noted 'book-book' call of the Boobook Owl *(Ninox novaeseelandiae)*. Most typically it is a bird of woodlands, where trees are large enough to provide roosting or nesting hollows, but growth is sufficiently open, especially near the ground, to allow hunting. The Boobook drops to the ground to take mice, small native mammals, spiders, beetles or other insects, and sometimes captures small birds and large flying insects. This owl, Australia's most common, may be seen in coastal forests. It also inhabits desert regions wherever there are a few trees, or where cliff crevices or caves substitute for tree hollows as nest sites.

Right: Australia has several species of blue-tongue lizards, between them covering most of Australia. They have rather bulky bodies, and legs that seem rather inadequate so that the body usually slides across the ground. When alarmed, blue-tongues gape wide, displaying the unusual bright tongue colour, which may deter some predators, although in fact blue-tongues are completely harmless. Best known of the genus must be the Eastern Blue-tongue, of coastal northern and eastern forests. Shown here is the Western Blue-tongue *(Tiliqua occipitalis)* which inhabits spinifex, mulga and mallee country. Its distribution is from western New South Wales and north-western Victoria through drier parts of South Australia and the Northern Territory around to Western Australia.

Left: One of the most widespread of trees in the woodlands of south-western Australia, the Salmon Gum *(Eucalyptus salmonophloia),* reaches a substantial size even in areas of low rainfall. Its smooth bark is generally a pale salmon colour, often deeper-coloured in autumn, while the very glossy deep green foliage forms a high umbrella crown. Woodlands characteristically have widely spaced trees. Usually the height of the treetrunks up to the first branches of the crown, is less than the height from lowest to highest foliage in the crown. Conversely, with forest trees, the crown occupies less than half of the total height. Salmon gums are tall and long-trunked, like forest trees, but with scattered foliage canopy. In some parts of Australia, grasses form the ground cover in woodlands; elsewhere, there are small shrubs without any grass. This forms a most important habitat for birds and mammals.

Left: One of Australia's most familiar small birds, the Willie Wagtail *(Rhipidura leucophyrs),* is restlessly active and inquisitive. Except in rainforests and totally treeless regions, this bird occurs almost everywhere and its distribution covers the whole continent except Tasmania. An erratic side-to-side twist of the body when perched, or on the ground, causes the long tail to swing almost constantly from side to side in a wide arc. Insects, spiders and other small creatures are taken from foliage, the ground, or caught in the air. The nest is constructed of grass, so bound together with spiders' webs that it has a felt-like consistency. The Willie Wagtail is renowned for fearless defence of its nest.

Right: Flying in to its neatly constructed nest, a female Scarlet Robin *(Petroica multicolor)* displays plumage that, while lacking the bold bright scarlet and black of the male, is still very attractive. Scarlet Robins are birds of open forests and woodlands, extending from south-eastern Queensland through eastern New South Wales and Victoria to Tasmania and South Australia. A separate population inhabits the south-west corner of Western Australia. Scarlet Robins are among Australia's best-known small birds, often visiting parks and gardens. The male feeds the female while she is brooding the eggs, and assists in feeding the young.

Left: Through the silvered limbs of sub-alpine woodlands can be seen the flat-topped blue silhouette of Mt. Olympus. Below, there is a small lake in the valley. These eucalypts are growing close to the upper limit of tree growth on Mt. Rufus in Tasmania's Cradle Mountain-Lake St. Clair National Park. In these high altitude woodlands most of the treetops are dead, bleached stark white by the harsh winter environment, when ice and snow cover the landscape for many months. Above this level the trees very abruptly thin out, and reach no higher up the mountain. Further down they are replaced by rainforests and the tall close-packed giants of the wet eucalypt forests. There are as many birds in these high woodlands as in the lower rainforests, for here the sunlight penetrates, allowing a diversity of shrubs and foraging niches.

Left: Probably the most bizarre of Australia's small reptiles is the ant-eating Thorny or Mountain Devil *(Moloch horridus)*. Apart from the rather alarming appearance, with spines, humps and bright colours, the 'Devil' has other, probably more remarkable, characteristics. For any creature of arid regions, or of habitats with hot dry summers, the ability to soak up water through its skin is valuable. A Thorny Devil placed in shallow water soon becomes very moist all over, as the water is soaked up, as if by blotting paper. The water is not absorbed through the skin, but passes into tiny capillary channels that lead eventually to the mouth, where the water is swallowed. Also of survival value is the Thorny Devil's ability to change its colour by varying the strength of skin pigmentation, becoming brighter or dull, to effectively match the soil or rocks of its habitat. The Moloch, as it is also commonly known, is found in central and western parts of the continent, in arid spinifex and mulga, mallee, and some temperate woodlands.

Previous page: Sub-alpine woodlands surround Lake Hanson, on the Cradle Mountain plateau of Tasmania. During the most intensive period of glaciation this region was covered by glaciers which gouged out the basins now occupied by Crater Lake, Lake Dove and Lake Hanson. This view from the slopes of Cradle Mountain is across Lake Hanson in its woodland valley, to the Huon River Valley, and beyond that to the plateau of the Central Highlands. Towards the upper limits of tree growth the Tasmanian sub-alpine woodlands have stunted but picturesque trees, of several species. A number of red-flowered shrubs grow in the woodland undergrowth, including the Honey Richea *(Richea scoparia)*, the Tasmanian Waratah *(Telopea truncata)*, Tasmanian Snow Berries *(Cyathodes juniperma)* and the Pandani *(Richea pandanifolia)*.

Left: At first glance this lizard appears to be legless, having a superficially snake-like appearance. On close examination, however, it will be seen to have vestigial limbs, tiny and flattened like paddles, normally lying flat, but occasionally held out at right angles to the body. The Sharp-snouted lizard has established itself in a wide variety of habitats, from the deserts of the interior to the coastal forests. Its distribution extends from southern Australia to New Guinea. There are many differing colour and pattern variations, but the pointed snout is very distinctive. Common is a grey form, with a herring-bone pattern, or longitudinal stripes. A form from northern Queensland is golden yellow with dark stripes.

Above: The Grey Butcher-bird (*Cracticus torquatus*) inhabits a wide variety of wooded country throughout Australia, excluding the northern, largely treeless, desert belt and Cape York Peninsula. Butcher-birds are among the most deadly predators upon small birds of the Australian bushland, probably more so than hawks and kookaburras, and are often responsible for the robbing of nests. But this is part of the overall balance of nature in the bush, and explains why such birds as the robins and wrens must raise several broods in each season. Within a few days of having a nest robbed by a predator they will be busily building a new nest nearby. Butcher-birds, of which there are four species, derive this name from their butcher-like habit of impaling their prey on a twig or wedging it into a fork to tear it apart.

COASTS AND ISLAND SANCTUARIES

The nest of the White-breasted Sea-eagle, a massive flat-topped pile of sticks on a cliff ledge, commanded a view of deep blue, white-flecked ocean; below near the foot of the cliffs the breakers rolled in across shallow reefs, the water alternately foaming white, then crystal clear, making visible every detail of rock, seaweed and sand of the seabed. Through these clear shallows could be seen occasionally the bulky oval shapes of turtles, sea lions and porpoises. On rocky parts of the shore, Sooty Oyster-catchers probed the crevices for limpets and mussels, while further along on a small sandy beach a pair of Pied Oyster-catchers guarded their eggs on the sand.

On the big nest on the cliff ledge, two young sea-eagles, almost ready to fly, exercised their wings, facing into the wind, holding wings outstretched, so that the strong gusts lifted them, for a moment, just a little above the nest. Soon they would be soaring with their parents, the sleek white and black shapes that soared high overhead, patrolling the island coastline.

As the sun moved lower these cliffs cast long shadows across the beach, bringing an early twilight. From the sand-dune scrub a small animal moved out on to the beach — a tiny Barred Bandicoot, pausing every now and then to dig, then probe in the sand with long-pointed snout.

The Australian coasts and islands have their own distinct flora and fauna. The coasts encompass a great variety of habitats, ranging from rocky coasts and sandy beaches, to tidal mudflats and mangrove swamps.

The shores and islands are a meeting place between the fauna of land and ocean. On the island beaches may be seen basking Sea Lions, but also land mammals such as the Barred Bandicoot.

The islands around Australia have become extremely important in fauna conservation, as sanctuaries for important species. On the Australian mainland many of the small marsupials, which in the early days of European settlement were common, have become extinct, or extremely rare. On the islands only, where those destructive, introduced predators, the foxes and cats have not become established, some of the small native mammals are able to survive.

Outstanding, as offshore fauna sanctuaries, are Bernier Island, Dorre Island and Barrow Island, situated off the north-western coast. Here the Barred Bandicoot is still common, although extremely rare on the mainland where once it was abundant.

The Banded Hare-wallaby and the Boodie, a rat-kangaroo, are both common on these islands, but extremely rare elsewhere. The Quokka, another small rat-kangaroo, is abundant on Rottnest Island near Perth, but scarce on the mainland where it was plentiful until the 1930s.

On the Pearson Islands, off the coast of South Australia at the eastern end of the Great Australian Bight, a rock wallaby occurs, *Petrogale penicillata pearsoni.* Isolated here, it has evolved as a sub-species different from the mainland rock-wallabies and is unique to these islands.

Other islands around Australia are renowned for their abundance of sea birds. Heron Island, in the Capricorn Group on Queensland's Barrier Reef, is noted for its multitude of birds. Among the branches of the island's stunted trees are nesting colonies of White-capped Noddies, while Wedge-tail Mutton-birds nest in burrows, in great numbers. Cormorants, Sandpipers, Oyster-catchers, and other sea birds are common. Six species of tern nest on the islands of the Capricorn Group: the Crested Tern, the Lesser Crested Tern, the Black-naped Tern, the Bridled Tern, the Roseate Tern, and the Little Tern.

The many islands of Bass Strait are important as fauna sanctuaries, some with seal colonies, many with sea-bird rookeries. Islands of the Furneaux Group are breeding grounds of the Cape Barren Goose, and for the Short-tailed Shearwater or Mutton-bird. Cat Island has a small number of Australian Gannet, the remains of two large breeding colonies that once numbered many thousands of birds. Albatross Island, north-west of the Hunter Group, accommodates one of only two Albatross rookeries in Australian waters.

The major west-coastal bird islands are those of the Abrolhos group. A cluster of low sand and limestone hummocks surrounded by extensive coral reefs, most of these islands have some low scrub and mangrove trees. They provide the main refuge and breeding place for thousands of sea birds of the Western Australian coast. There are several species of Shearwater and many Terns, and the Lesser Noddy and the Shag breed are prevalent on some islands. The Abrolhos Tammar Wallaby, an island subspecies, occurs on two of the islands, while White-breasted Sea-eagles and Osprey are still common.

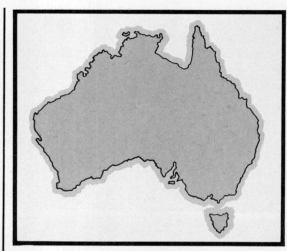

A few species of land birds on these islands appear sensitive to human interference, and may be in danger of extinction; these include island varieties of the Scrub Wren and the Painted Quail.

The tropical mangrove swamps form a totally different coastal environment. The mangrove trees are massed together in marine mudflats, a habitat which attracts a great diversity of wildlife. The most notorious inhabitant is the Saltwater Crocodile.

A strange small denizen of the mudflats of the far north is the Mudskipper, a fish which can leave the water and walk on the mud, and even climb trees. It is surprisingly fast out of the water, paddling along on its fins, or skipping away from a pursuer with a powerful flick of its tail.

The mangroves have a rich birdlife, with many species found only in mangrove swamps. Among these are the Mangrove Whistler, Mangrove Bittern, Mangrove Robin and Mangrove Kingfisher.

Opposite page: The late afternoon sunlight gives a gold-burnished gleam to the heavy swell of the Southern Ocean, as it rolls into a bay below the cliffs of Cape Beaufort. Australia's southern coastline west of the Great Australian Bight is one of sandy beaches with large scrub-covered dunes alternating with rocky headlands.

Left: Bold black-and-white plumage, crimson eye and bill make the Pied Oystercatcher (*Haematopus ostralegus*) a most attractive bird. It frequents sandy beaches and coastal mudflats around the entire Australian coastline, and is most common in Tasmania. The shoreline environs are shared between this bird, and the similar but all-black Sooty Oystercatcher, which, however, keeps to stony beaches and wave platform areas. The Pied Oystercatcher feeds by probing deeply with its long straight bill into sand or mud for marine worms, sea snails and cockles. On its rocky sections of coast, the Sooty Oystercatcher prises or hammers open mussels and limpets. Both species nest on the beaches, the Pied laying its eggs in a slight hollow in the sand, the Sooty among stones. With each species the freckled coloration of the eggs makes detection difficult. The birds are very wary, and slip off the nest when any intruder is still at a great distance.

Left: Found throughout Australia wherever suitable areas of water exist, the Pelican *(Pelecanus conspicillatus)* utilizes both fresh and saltwater habitats, ranging from tidal mudflats to temporary desert lakes. Pelicans are impressive as they lumber into flight from the water with powerful slow-beating wings, or when they glide in, to splash down like seaplanes. Equally fascinating is a group fishing, swimming in formation, thrusting their heads deep down beneath the water, often all in unison, then bringing their huge bills up together. Nesting occurs in large colonies, usually on small islands which afford protection from predators. Breeding will occur after rain has created suitable conditions, and not until the bird is at least four years of age. When breeding commences in the Pelican colony, the mature birds develop courtship colours, the forward part of the pouch beneath the bill darkening from pink to red. Both birds together construct the nest, and each takes turn to incubate the two eggs while the other is away feeding. Pelican colonies are easily disturbed, and careless intrusion can cause mass desertions of nests.

Above: A coastline of beaches and rugged headlands is situated at the foot of the Mt. Barren Range, in the Fitzgerald River National Park. This is a remote and fairly inaccessible part of the continent's southern coast, and has remained a magnificent wilderness area. Two broad river estuaries, that of the Fitzgerald and the Demster, reach the ocean in this bay, their still waters separated from the ocean surf by only a sand bar. On the sheltered estuary and sand bar are usually large numbers of Stilts, Avocets, Black Swans, and often, Mountain Ducks. This ocean beach is a habitat for Pied Oyster-catchers, various terns, gulls and dotterels.

Following page: Grotesque black silhouettes of pandanas palms at sunrise frame a scene of golden beaches and headlands at Noosa, Queensland. The pandanus is characteristic of the northern Australian coasts, where it gives an atmosphere of tropical luxuriance. This small area around Noosa contains a considerable diversity of habitat, both land and marine. On the hills of the headland there are small pockets of rainforest, and areas of heath with a variety of coastal wildflowers. To the north of Noosa Heads in Lagoona Bay, a long sweep of wide beach extends to Cooloola, where coloured sandhills several hundred metres high are preserved within a national park. Behind this beach are several lakes, into which flow the Noosa River and some creeks. Inland are the unusual Glasshouse Mountains, which can be seen from the ocean. Along this southern part of the Queensland coast the islands are of sand-dune formation, best known at Fraser Island, but also at Bribie Island, North Stradbroke and Moreton Islands. Further north the character of the Queensland coast changes, becoming more rugged, and the islands are totally different, being steep tops of submerged ranges.

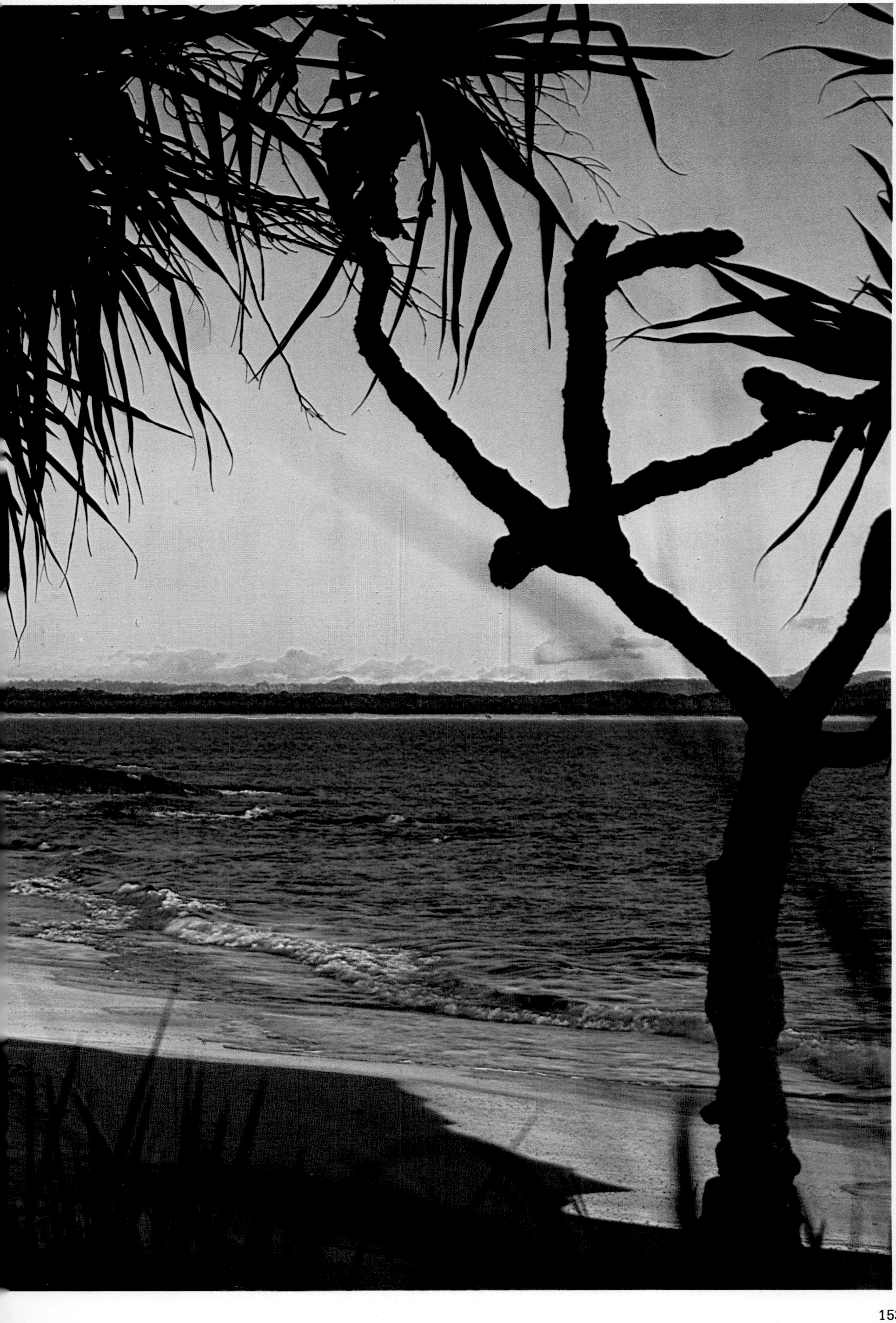

Left: The small land hermit crab of tropical Australian beaches is a fascinating study in modification to suit special needs. The most obvious adaptation is the alteration of its body shape, compared with other crabs, to suit the tapering internal shape of the shell. Details of modification are in evidence elsewhere. When alarmed it withdraws into its shell, but not completely: the legs cannot be accommodated inside, and so remain out, but tightly packed together to form a barricade. For this purpose the segments of the legs have become almost triangular in cross-section, and their flattened sides pack together. The surface thus presented to the hostile outside world is hemispherical, and the legs themselves form a spherical surface like the triangular cross-sectioned segments of an orange. Land crabs such as this *Coenobita* species are able to live indefinitely out of water, but generally remain at the wave-washed edge of the sea.

Right: Australia has three species of sea birds known as 'noddies', these being the Common Noddy, the White-capped Noddy and the Lesser Noddy. The Common Noddy has the widest distribution, around the coastline of the northern half of the continent. The White-capped Noddy frequents islands off the Queensland coast. By comparison the slightly smaller Lesser Noddy *(Anous tenuirostris)* has an extremely restricted contact with the Australian coastline. This is a bird of the oceans, and has only two known breeding grounds, the Seychelles Islands in the Indian Ocean, and the Abrolhos group of islands, just off the Western Australian coast near Geraldton. Here the Lesser Noddies roost and nest in flocks of thousands, covering the mangroves of island lagoons with their nests. These are extremely solid structures of seaweed cemented together with the birds' white lime-like excrement. During the nesting season, from August to January, these birds sit very tightly, even to the extent that some must be lifted from their nests to inspect eggs or young.

Right: Although similar in long-nosed, big-eared appearance to the Rabbit-eared Bandicoot, this Little Marl or Barred Bandicoot *(Perameles bougainville)* is far smaller. Once common across much of mainland Australia, this harmless little marsupial is now reduced to a very few small colonies. It is reasonably common only on several island sanctuaries. On Bernier Island, some 50 km out from Australia's mid-western coast, these tiny bandicoots emerge towards evening from their burrows among dense low coastal scrub, to forage along the beaches, digging in the sand for insects or other small creatures. Until the coming of European man, his foxes, cats and other introduced animals, the Little Marl was abundant in western New South Wales, western Victoria, southern parts of South Australia, and the southern half of Western Australia. Now, apart from the island sanctuaries, there have been records of its existence only in Victoria.

Left: Australia's common seagull, the Silver Gull *(Larus novaehollandiae),* occurs around almost the entire coastline, and throughout the inland except for the most arid of desert areas. Gulls are gregarious scavengers of seas, shores, rivers and lakes, feeding on almost everything found to be edible. At times they form floating rafts of large numbers of birds, feeding on surface debris, often the refuse of fishing boats. Gulls are familiar as scavengers of beaches and coastal parks, and descend upon city rubbish dumps in huge numbers. This last habit makes them, in some localities, a problem as actual or potential carriers of disease to other water birds, and to otherwise clean lakes. Silver Gulls usually choose to nest on small islands, preferably where low-growing vegetation gives the colony of birds a clear view of any approaching predator. The nest is a shallow bowl of sticks, seaweed or other local plant debris; two or three, sometimes four brownish, black-patterned eggs are laid. Nesting dates vary, most colonies being active either in spring or autumn, but some breeding in both seasons.

Right: Ocean swells break with full force against low limestone cliffs. Undiminished by any reef or islands, their pounding force has cut back the land, but left the rock beneath sea level as a broad wave platform. In rough weather this is a wide expanse of churning foam, but when seas are slight and the tide low, it is often possible to walk on the exposed rock of such wave-cut ledges. In the pools may be seen the bright coral structures, colourful crabs, sea urchins and other marine life. The shore birds also work their way over the exposed rocks. Sooty Oystercatchers, specialists of rocky coasts, prise open the oysters and mussels. In some places small islets, rock pinnacles rising from the submerged wave-platform, are used by Ospreys and White-breasted Sea-eagles as safe places to build their bulky nests.

Left: Young White-breasted Sea-eagles, almost ready to leave the nest, try their wings by facing into the strong breeze blowing in from the sea, allowing themselves to be lifted momentarily from the nest. If the gust is too strong they are quick to fold their wings and drop safely on to the wide pile of sticks. At other times, when there is not enough wind for this game, the young eagles will run across the flat-topped nest, flapping wings and jumping into the air, to gain a moment of flight. From their vantage point on a cliff ledge, the sea-eagles command a panoramic view each way along this rugged island coast; far below the ocean breaks on to reefs, partly submerged wave-platforms, and beaches. From this height, the clear water reveals the wealth of island marine life. Apart from the large sea creatures, the seals, porpoises and turtles, their sharp eyes locate and follow schools of fish, and even big crayfish moving slowly across the seabed. Along the shores, they watch oystercatchers, gulls and other birds. Often the young eagles turn their gaze to the sky, and their incredibly acute vision will follow movements that the human can locate only after much scanning of the sky with binoculars. Mostly they watch for their parents, which from below look rather like huge gulls, white-plumaged, black wing-tips, and rather short tails. The White-breasted Sea-eagle *(Haliaeetus leucogaster)* occurs almost all around the Australian coastline, as well as along many major rivers such as the Murray, and on some of the large lakes near the coast. Its nest is a huge pile of sticks, several metres across, generally in a high secure position.

A bull Sea Lion at very close quarters is probably the most awe-inspiring of Australian mammals. It is certainly the most massive, its bulky body exceeding 3 m in length. Sea Lions come ashore on secluded beaches at a number of places around Australia's southern coastline, usually on offshore islands. Here they seem to spend most of their time basking in the sun, spread out on sand or flat rocks enjoying what seems an idyllic life. Only when very closely approached will the bulls raise themselves threateningly, and perhaps lunge forward; the far smaller females, if accompanied by pups, are always prepared to launch a sudden attack. The Australian Sea Lion *(Neophoca cinerea)* is one of the hair-seal group; soon after birth the young lose their fine dense under-fur, retaining only the coarse hair coat. The Australian Sea Lion is a creature of Australia's southern oceans, from South Australia's Kangaroo Island, around the Great Australian Bight to Cape

Leeuwin and up the west coast as far as the Abrolhos Islands. The colonies keep to island rather than mainland beaches, but mainland colonies do exist. In spite of their awkward lumbering appearance, Sea Lions can move quite fast across a beach, and are surprisingly agile in climbing over boulders. They have scaled steep rocky slopes and have on occasions been reported quite a few kilometres inland. The sudden emerging of a bull Sea Lion from the reeds of some placid little inland waterhole could well have been the origin of bunyip legends. Often the Sea Lions, particularly the small sleek females, will swim curiously around small boats visiting the islands, and in the water they are, in complete contrast, swift and graceful.

Sea Lions are members of the large order Carnivora, the non-marsupial carnivores. Australia has very few species of this order: with the exception of the Dingo, native carnivorous mammals are marsupials.

Within the Carnivora, there are two families of seals, of which four species may be seen around Australian coasts. The Sea Lion is known as a hair seal, because the fine dense under-fur is lost when very young, leaving only a hair coat. Two species of the smaller fur seals visit Australian coasts and islands, and were the basis of a fur industry when thousands were killed each year on the Bass Strait islands. The Australian Fur Seal occurs from New South Wales to Victoria and Tasmania, while the New Zealand Fur Seal visits shores of South Australia and Western Australia. The Elephant Seal occasionally appears on or near Australian coasts; a massive mammal much larger than the Sea Lion, it reaches 5 or 6 m in length. One of the family known as earless or true seals, Elephant Seals are more completely adapted to marine life than other seals. Their hind-limbs, resembling the tail-fins of fish, are even more awkard than usual on land.

Right: The coastline of the Great Australian Bight is, along much of its length, one of cliffs, one part said to be the longest unbroken line of cliffs in the world. But at one section, where the escarpment curves inland, there is a low narrow coastal plain. Along this low sandy coast strong winds have built up big shifting dunes of white sand. The old overland telegraph station, built in 1877, and long abandoned, is now partly buried by these dunes. Under the cliffs of this southern edge of the continent are thought to be the exits of some of the cave systems that extend far beneath the Nullarbor. These well known caves have crater-like pothole entrances on the flat surface of the Nullarbor, and extend into huge cathedral-like caverns, with lakes and underground streams that may eventually reach the ocean beneath the cliffs.

Left: At Shark Bay, virtually the westernmost part of Australia, in the shallow, tidal, almost landlocked region of extensive mudflats at Hamelin Pool, the beach is of a peculiar rubbery mud. Just above the waterline, where still damp, this mud cracks into large blocks, of spongy texture, more like rubber than mud, being springy and resilient. From the mud along this shoreline emerge domes of what appears to be rather soft rock. These are a form of living rock, known as stromatolite. Until comparatively recent times, these structures were known only from past geological ages. The discovery of living stromatolites in the protected bay environment of Shark Bay, has made possible the study of the living algae that build these formations. The rubbery mudflats are an 'algal mat', consisting of unicellular blue-green filamentous algae intermixed with sediments. When the mud algae mat cracks into blocks, some of these blocks are enlarged by algae and sediment deposits by the sea, to produce growing domes.

Right: The mangrove belt that skirts much of the Australian coastline is one of its richest wildlife habitats, with inhabitants ranging from massive Saltwater Crocodiles to tiny hermit crabs. Mangrove forests have reached their greatest development in the great number of silted river estuaries and sheltered bays with tidal mudflats around the northern Australian coastline. 'Mangrove' is the name for a number of species of trees that have adapted to live in the tidal shallows, where almost constant waterlogging and high salt concentrations would kill other trees. The mangrove trees have a number of adaptations, including buttress-like aerial roots. The various species specialise within this habitat, some growing only in the deeper seaward edge of the mangrove belt, others only on the higher landward side. A great variety of wildlife is dependent upon mangrove vegetation.

MALLEE AND ARID WOODLANDS

The story of the mallee is one of adaptations of Australia's ubiquitous eucalypts for survival, in regions of low rainfall or poor soil. In rich moist coastal soils, species of eucalypt can soar to heights around 100 metres but cannot survive bushfires. By contrast, for the arid regions, other species of eucalypt have evolved that grow to a mere 3 or 4 metres height, and can recover from fire.

'Mallee' is the name given to a specific pattern of growth among the eucalypts, particularly those of arid regions, and other places where rigorous conditions prevail. Each small tree has a cluster of slender stems arising from the ground. The buried base, which forms the junction between stems and roots, is a massive knotted rootstock. At this growth centre, stems rise upwards, roots go down and outwards.

To obtain moisture, the mallee trees have deep taproots, but other finer roots spread outwards, to take advantage of surface moisture. Even the dew of the cold inland night can be gathered. The leaves of these trees, waxy-surfaced, hang downwards; dew or light misty rain on the leaves soon drips from their fine points, wetting the sand beneath their low spreading foliage canopy. The moisture of the soil, whether from dew or rain, is conserved by the mallee habit of growth. Between the upright stems becomes wedged a mass of twigs, strips of bark and leaves, some fallen from above, some wind-blown and entangled. A clump of mallee-bush, like a wire mesh fence, collects and holds all debris.

But it is this litter layer that further assists survival. The soil into which the foliage drips, from rain or dew, is shaded and sheltered from wind by its dense mulch layer. The shallow surface roots that capture these small amounts of moisture, which would never be sufficient to reach down to the deep roots, are kept cool. In dense mallee stands, almost the entire ground surface, between as well as beneath the trees, becomes a debris layer, retaining precious moisture, keeping the ground cooler. Above, the foliage makes an almost continuous low canopy.

The hardwood of fallen twigs and stems, and the fallen but tough leaves, decay only very slowly in the dry climate. This debris layer builds up over the years, until a fire is started, if not by man then by lightning strike. Fuelled by the accumulated and usually tinder-dry debris, the fire is

likely to be fierce, igniting the foliage of the mallee canopy, and totally destroying the standing vegetation; usually only blackened sticks remain.

Unlike the trunks of most other eucalypts, these stems do not as a rule sprout fresh buds and foliage after fire. New shoots, long dormant in that bulky rootstock, come to life, and the new stems grow rapidly from the sand beside the blackened sticks of the old mallee. The same happens when the land is cleared. Mallee scrub knocked down regrows rapidly, unless the mallee roots are ripped from the earth.

A fresh supply of nutrients from the litter layer is contained in the ashbeds of the fire. Seeds of the mallee eucalypts, and of other plants, are released. Hakeas for example, have their seeds enclosed in hard woody capsules, which after fire split open, and drop the seeds in the ashbeds.

Seedlings would stand little chance in mature mallee scrub; the dense litter layer of the crowded scrub smothers out new plants. But on the open ground cleared by fire, plants of a multitude of genera and species appear.

A year after fire, in mallee country, an abundance of small herbaceous wildflowers clothe the wasteland, and the new mallee stems have started to shoot upwards. Five years later, the wildflowers have been suppressed by the massed new mallees spreading above. The mallee scrub is mature after ten to fifteen years. The ground retains few small plants, but has a dense litter layer.

There are many national parks where mallee country, its unique wildflowers and animal life, can be seen. Mallee country extends from south-western New South Wales and western Victoria, across much of South Australia, to the southern parts of Western Australia.

Some of the most famous of mallee reserves are in Victoria. Wyperfeld National Park 400 km north-west of Melbourne, is one of Victoria's largest national parks. Here on the Wimmera River System, the dominant vegetation is of mallee eucalypts on old sand dune country. One of the common species is the Yellow Mallee, which extends into South Australia. In spring months this sandy mallee country has many wildflowers, particularly in open heath-like openings between dense mallee patches. These include the Papery Sunray, the Orange Immortelle, and the Poached-egg Daisy. Wyperfeld was dedicated a park for the purpose of preserving the unique flora and fauna,

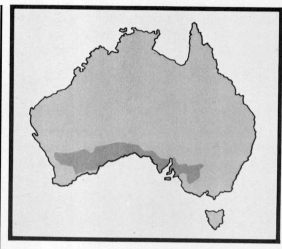

including the Mallee Fowl or Lowan. Flora includes the Red Mallee, the Congoo Mallee, the Quandong and the Weeping Pittosporum. Among smaller wildflowers are Violet Honey Myrtle, Heath Myrtle, Crimson Mint-bush and Correa.

Well known also in south-eastern Australia is the Little Desert National Park. This is part of an extensive region of sandy mallee country along Victoria's border with South Australia; to its north is a larger mallee area, known as Big Desert.

Many of South Australia's national parks and reserves are of mallee habitat, including Lincoln National Park, Hincks, and Hambidge on the Eyre Peninsula. In the south-east of that state, mallee occurs in Billiat, Mt. Rescue, Messent and Scorpion Springs Conservation Parks.

Western Australia has a major mallee area reserved in the Lake Magenta National Park, in the southern interior.

Opposite page: Many areas of arid woodlands are quite well vegetated with rather stunted and gnarled eucalypts, acacia trees and other shrubs. The ground typically has a considerable layer of accumulated litter under the trees, interspersed with large areas of bare earth.

Left: Shrike-thrushes are among the most melodious of the birds of the Australian bush, with clear, varied and pleasantly musical calls, which compensate for their lack of plumage colours. The bird pictured is flying into a nest hidden in a hollow stump. The name 'shrike-thrush' is given to these birds because they were considered once to be related to both shrikes and thrushes; they are sometimes known simply as 'thrushes'. Some are restricted to tropical northern and north-eastern coastal areas, but one species has a very wide distribution across the entire continent except for some extreme desert areas. This is the Grey Thrush *(Colluricincla harmonica),* of which there are three variations, inhabiting eastern Australia, northern Australia, and the central and western regions. These are often known as the Grey, the Brown and the Western Shrike-thrush respectively.

Right: The Mallee Honeyeater, or Yellow-plumed Honeyeater *(Meliphaga ornatus)* is one of the most conspicuous of the birds of the mallee and arid woodlands. Though not brightly coloured, these birds attract attention by their noisy activities in the treetops, vigorously chasing, squabbling, chattering, as they feed among the leaves. At first light of day, well before sunrise, the loud, ringing, cheerful dawn chorus of honeyeaters awakens the bushland, and throughout the day they are among the most abundant and conspicuously active of birds. This honeyeater occurs in north-western Victoria, south-western New South Wales, and southern districts of South Australia and Western Australia. The rather fragile-looking nest is delicately suspended from its rim in the outer foliage of a tree or shrub.

Left: Of the many wrens that inhabit Australia, three species share the characteristic of having reddish 'shoulders'. Most widespread of these, the Variegated Wren, is found from eastern to western coasts. Although similar in appearance, the other two species are of very restricted distribution; these are the Red-winged Wren, and the Blue-breasted Wren. This last species, the Blue-breasted *(Malurus pulcherrimus)* shown here, has a broken distribution from south-western Australia, to Eyre Peninsula in South Australia. This habitat is of mallee, temperate woodlands, dry open forests and heathlands. The male Blue-breasted Wren is readily distinguished from the Variegated by its deep blue instead of black breast, recognised only in bright light. It is harder to distinguish from the Red-winged Wren of the same habitat, with a very dark, almost black breast. Fortunately the calls are distinctive.

Previous page: The slender multiple trunks of mallee eucalypts form a dark lattice work against white cliffs. These trees grow from slopes littered with fallen stems and twigs. It is typical of mallee country, that the part of the tree that is above ground is disposable, and dies in fire or severe drought. The rootstock however, remains beneath the ground, and sends fast-growing new stems up, to reach full height within a few years. This mallee, *Eucalyptus annulata,* turns bright yellow as the old bark peels away at the end of summer. The fallen dead stems, the previous growth from the same rootstock, lie among the accumulated debris of twigs, bark and leaves. These build up as a dense layer especially around the base of the tree, shading and keeping cooler the ground above the roots conserving moisture. Mallee vegetation is the preferred habitat of the Mallee Fowl and the Mallee Kangaroo.

Above: Probably the most common of Australia's small hawks is the Nankeen Kestrel *(Falco cenchroides).* Unlike many others of the falcon family, this bird does not hunt by speed of pursuit, but hovers above the ground until some small creature, a mouse, small lizard, spider or insect is spotted. The Kestrel drops like a falling stone, to

plunge, talons outstretched, into the grass to take its prey. A hovering Kestrel is fascinating to watch; even on a windy day it can maintain its exact location in the air. While its wings flutter and its tail twists for control, its head alone remains motionless, fixed in one exact unchanging position, while the sharp eyes watch for movement below. The Nankeen Kestrel is found almost throughout Australia, in open woodlands, and in treeless shrublands and grasslands where holes in cliffs are used for nesting. Here a Kestrel comes in to its nest in a large hollow, where its young, almost large enough to fly, excitedly await the arrival of food.

Right: Bright pink flower heads make *Melaleuca steedmanii* one of the most attractive of the melaleucas. This low shrub of Western Australia often grows around or in crevices of granite outcrops, in the usually sparse undergrowth of temperate or semi-arid woodlands.

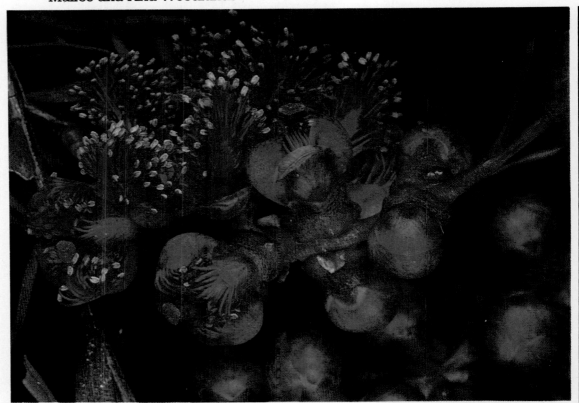

Right: Long radiating bud-caps, and fused-together seed capsules make the Bushy Yate an unusual tree. Its bright light green colour, although sometimes yellow or white, is also uncommon. The Bush Yate *(Eucalyptus lehmanii)* is a small thin-stemmed mallee or tree which flowers between July and January, and occurs along the south coast of Western Australia.

Right: The group of wildflowers of the genus *Dryandra,* consisting of some 60 species, is found only in south-western Australia. This rare species, the King Dryandra *(Dryandra proteoides)* grows on stony ridges, where there is a rather stunted woodland or mallee vegetation. The flower heads of dryandras consist of a central cluster of many small flowers, surrounded by the overlapping layers of armour-like and usually colourful bracts, which in the bud stage completely cover the flowers.

Previous page: The Murchison is a typical river of semi-arid inland regions of the southern half of this continent, and flows through a variety of country. Its mouth is on Australia's western coast south of Shark Bay. The lower reaches of the river flow through the colourful Kalbarri Gorge entrenched into sandplain country. Further inland, most of its course is through alternating and intermixed areas of mulga and arid woodlands. In some regions the river itself creates its own patches of arid woodland, where it has broad floodplain flats. In these places white-trunked River Gums *(Eucalyptus camaldulensis)* form a sparse open woodland along the river, in some places extending a few kilometres away from the river. These River Gums are very stunted in growth and gnarled in shape, compared with the River Gums that grow in the permanently moist soils of river beds and banks. But for bird life, the arid woodlands that occur as small patches in regions of low scrub, and especially woodlands near rivers, are greatly favoured habitats. The birds, particularly the parrots, cockatoos, hawks and eagles, are attracted both by the river pools, and by the trees as nesting sites.

Above: Through vast tracts of mallee, woodland and mulga scrub country of inland Australia, the clear strong call of the Crested Bellbird is a distinctive part of the character of this country. The calls have no resemblance to those of the east-coastal bellbirds, which are Bell Miners. Those birds, actually honeyeaters, have a metallic tink-tink call, repeated almost endlessly. The call of the Crested Bellbird closely resembles the sound of an old-fashioned cow bell in the distance, a deeper sound, of unevenly spaced notes. The Crested Bellbird*(Oreoica gutturalis)* is widely distributed from inland New South Wales, Queensland and Victoria through South Australia and the Northern Territory to parts of Western Australia.

Left: Mallee eucalypts on Eyre Peninsula, South Australia are seen through early morning mist. Visible are the multiple trunks, low-branching habit of growth, and low foliage crown of the mallee eucalypt. Some mallee species have quite thick stems, and make trees of 6 or 8 m tall, others have stems of finger thickness, and fully grown stand only at a height of 2 or 3 m. South Australia has very extensive areas of mallee vegetation, covering most of Eyre Peninsula, and much of the inland south-east, where it extends into north-western Victoria.

Right: One of the more common geckos, the species *Heteronotia binoei* is sufficiently well known to have acquired the common name of Prickly Gecko, and is also known as Bynoe's Gecko. Its extremely wide distribution covers the entire continent except the heavily forested and colder south-east and south-west. Within so extensive a distribution, the Prickly Gecko occupies a great variety of habitats, from wet coastal forests to central deserts. During the day it hides in rock crevices or beneath stones, bark, or other ground debris, emerging at night to feed upon small insects.

Left: Probably the richest outpouring of song likely to be heard in dry or temperate woodlands is that of the Rufous Songlark *(Cinclorhamphus mathewsi)*. It is in spring that this joyous singing becomes so overwhelming; outside the breeding season these birds are quiet and inconspicuous. The Songlark is all the more noticeable for its nuptial flights, when it sings loudly as it flies on rapidly vibrating wings. Unlike the closely related Brown Songlark which inhabits open plains, the Rufous Songlark seems to prefer areas of open ground with scattered trees. The nest is built into a small hollow scratched in the ground at the base of a grass tussock or beside a log.

Right: The Red Kangaroo *(Megaleia rufa)* is extremely widely distributed over vast areas of inland Australia. It avoids coastal woodlands and forests, and is uncommon in the most arid desert country. The open spaces, the grasslands, mulga scrublands, and open arid woodlands of widely scattered trees with understorey of sparse low shrubbery, are typical of its haunts. These habitats are of low average rainfall, but more importantly, are subject to severe droughts. The Red Kangaroo can withstand considerable extremes of heat and water shortage and at such times ceases to breed. In many regions, stock water at dams and windmills provided by pastoralists have made this kangaroo more abundant. Lack of permanent water previously limited Red Kangaroo populations. But in other areas, previously the best of this kangaroo's habitat, it no longer occurs. More than any other Australian native creature, the 'big red' has been the centre of conservation controversy.

Left: Areas of arid woodland with trees larger than low mallee of mulga shrubs, occur far out into the dry regions, often only in small patches or belts. White-bleached dead trees and golden wattles against bold inland colours of red earth and clear blue skies make this habitat colourful. There the diversity of wildlife increases, especially birdlife. In country such as this such birds could be expected as the Red-capped Robin, Mulga Parrot, Goshawk, Cinnamon Quail-thrush, Owlet Nightjar, Boobook Owl, Red-tailed Black Cockatoo, Kestrel, Crested Bellbird, Whiteface, Hooded Robin, Emu, Budgerigar, Bourke Parrot, Galah, Brown Hawk, Ring-necked Parrot, Spotted Harrier, Bee-eater, Spiny-cheeked Honeyeater, and Red-backed Kingfisher.

Left: Dunnarts are fierce little insect-hunters which stalk the Australian bush at night; so ferocious are they that they will attack and kill ordinary mice as large as themselves. The Fat-tailed Dunnart is the best-known of Australia's eleven species, as it is not only found in remote deserts, but inhabits woodlands, mallee and heathlands of south-eastern and south-western Australia. This is one of five dunnart species with fattened tails, which may provide a food reserve for poor seasons; of these, the Fat-tailed Dunnart *(Sminthopsis crassicaudata)* has been most intensively studied. Like some other small mammals, it is able to lower its body temperature in times of severe food shortage, or cold weather.

DRY EUCALYPT FORESTS

The dry eucalypt forests constitute one of the best known of Australian natural environments, because this type of forest occurs near most southern capitals. But no two localities of this, or any other segment of the natural environment, are identical in details of their vegetation, or their fauna; a visit to each new area holds fresh discoveries.

Forests differ from woodlands, principally in the closer spacing and larger size of their trees. Botanists have defined the difference more precisely: forests have tall trees whose bole height — the distance up to the first large branches — is greater than the distance from lowest branches to treetop.

Woodland trees, more widely spaced because of soil moisture limitations, receive an abundance of sunlight to the side foliage as well as to the highest parts of the crown. In this way the side foliage and low limbs are retained as equally useful. But with the closer spacing of forests, seen at its extreme in rainforests, the urgent need is to reach upwards. The side branches of saplings are discarded while small, in favour of growth directed to the uppermost foliage. The first branches permanently retained are those whose foliage reaches near the high canopy levels.

But unlike the very obvious, clear-cut boundary where eucalypt forest and rainforest meet, the transition from woodland to dry eucalypt forest can be so gradual as to be imperceptible. Very often, the same species of tree or trees which form a woodland in one locality will, in a nearby situation of slightly higher rainfall, slightly better soil, be taller, closer, and come within the definition of forest. But it would be difficult to pick the precise point at which the vegetation ceased to be woodland and became forest.

Birds and mammals of adjoining forests and woodlands likewise show considerable overlap.

Botanists describe Australian eucalypt forests as 'sclerophyllous', meaning hard-leaved, distinguishing them from the soft-leaved rainforests. The leaves of the sclerophyll forests have a thick outer cuticle which stiffens and protects them against the drying and burning of sun and hot winds.

Rainforest plants have large soft leaves with maximum areas devoted to achieving chlorophyll synthesis in subdued light. Without a humid environment, they are scorched and killed. In the shaded, crowded rainforest, a suitable climate is maintained.

Compared with the wet forests, the dry eucalypt forests have a more open canopy, lower trees, and grassy or low dry sclerophyllous scrub as ground cover. Ferns and epiphytes are generally absent.

Australia's dry forests tend to be located inland of the wet sclerophyll forests and rainforests of the south-east and south-west. In many drier parts of the coastline, dry sclerophyll forest reaches the coast, or frequently is separated from the sea by a strip of heathlands.

The dry eucalypt forests can be seen in many places within easy reach of Australia's major centres of population. Wide geographical separation may cause dry sclerophyll forests to be vastly different in species of plants. Their animal populations may also show considerable differences.

Around Sydney, dry eucalypt forests are an important segment of Ku-ring-gai Chase, Brisbane Waters, Dharug and Royal National Parks. On this sandstone country the dry forest trees are the Smooth-barked Apple, Sydney Peppermint, Red Bloodwood, Stringybark, and Scribbly Gum. Trees are well spaced, allowing the development of a dense shrub layer of which *Banksia serrata* and *Banksia spinulosa* are common, together with Sydney Boronia, Ledum Boronia and Pink-flowered Wax-plant.

Dry sclerophyll forest is the dominant vegetation of the Adelaide Hills and Mt. Lofty Ranges. At Belair National Park, two common trees are Messmate Stringybark, and Peppermint Box. Undergrowth includes Flame Heath, Tea-tree, Pink-flowered Fringe Myrtle and Needlebush.

Elsewhere in these ranges, as at Para Wira Recreation Park, the upper parts of the ranges have Long-leaved Box and Pink Gum. Further samples of the dry eucalypt forest and its undergrowth scrub, rich in wildflowers, is preserved at other national parks, such as Cleland and Morialta, each having its individual variation.

Perth has a great tract of forests along the Darling Ranges, bordering the suburbs and forming a green backdrop to the city. These forests are of dry sclerophyll, grading into woodlands further inland. The greater part is reserved for forestry and water catchment purposes, but there are some small national parks and forestry parks. A system of forestry Special Management Priority Areas preserves the vegetation of additional areas.

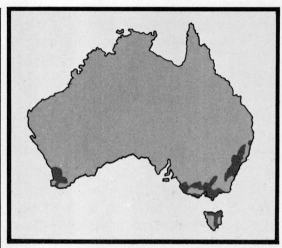

The Western Australian dry sclerophyll forests are dominated by Jarrah, with dark fibrous rough bark, and Wandoo, with smooth white bark. Jarrah forest can be seen along the highways that cut through the ranges to the east of the city, particularly the Albany Highway. The undergrowth scrub presents excellent wildflower displays from August to November, some prominent flowering species being the Bull Banksia, Wilson's Grevillea, Blue Lechenaultia, Urchin Dryandra, Hovea and Swan River Myrtle. Wandoo forest along the scarpland has Fuchsia Grevillea, Pincushion Coneflower, Large Hibbertia and Common Dampiera among its many hundreds of wildflowers.

Reserves in the forested ranges near Perth include John Forrest, Serpentine, Walyunga, Avon Valley, Greenmount, Kalamunda and Lesmurdie Falls National Parks.

Opposite page: The natural habitat of the Waratah *(Telopea speciosissima)* is the open forest of the top of the Gibraltar range, north-eastern New South Wales. This waratah is growing on a hillside spur of this area, overlooking valleys of the steep eastern escarpment of the Great Dividing Range.

177

Above: Almost the entire undersurface of the Flame Robin is a bright orange-red. Other red-breasted robins are either of deeper red or crimson, or of much more delicate pink tints, and no other has such an extensive red area. The Flame Robin *(Petroica phoenicea)* is confined to coastal south-eastern Australia, from the vicinity of Brisbane, to Adelaide, and is most common in Tasmania. In winter these birds may form small flocks, which break up in spring as pairs select nest territories. In mountain regions, nesting is late, after thawing of snowfields, around December and January. The nest is well camouflaged, generally tucked behind a piece of bark, or into a hollow.

Right: The Koala, probably more than any other Australian animal is the centre of popular affection, and is instantly and universally recognized at first glance. This animal is the result of a rather strange twist of evolution. Its very early ancestors were probably tree dwellers. But later ancestors were ground dwellers rather like the related wombats; during this time they gradually lost their tails. Finally this creature, now without the benefit the possums have of a grasping tail, returned again to the treetops. In addition, its pouch, which was rearward-opening as a ground animal, opens downwards now that it is a tree-climber. This could be disastrous for the young, but for the fact that it can be kept closed by muscular control. In compensation for the loss of the tail, the Koala has evolved long arms, powerful claws and a vice-like grip.

The Koala *(Phascolarctos cinereus)* is one of the most specialized of feeders, accepting only the leaves of a few of the smooth-barked species of eucalypts, and even some of these are unsuited at certain times of the year.

The Koala gives birth usually to a single young, which is carried on the female's back after 5 to 6 months in the pouch. Koalas are therefore slow breeders, probably averaging one young per year.

A heavily built, slow-moving marsupial, it is still fairly common in coastal Queensland south of Townsville. The Koala is now less common in New South Wales and Victoria. The first sighting was made in 1798 in the Blue Mountains. This report classified it as a sloth or a monkey, and the Koala was regarded as a bear until established as a marsupial.

Right and far right: The Feathertail Glider is the smallest of Australia's gliders. In Australia, flying mammals have evolved from several groups of marsupials. None of these animals can really fly, but rather they glide, and from a take-off point high on a tree can cover a considerable distance. In forests of tall trees with open spaces between the trunks, as in Australia's eucalypt forests and woodlands, gliding has great advantages. A small possum can travel from tree to tree without descending to the ground, where it could be easy prey for owls or other predators. Australia's gliders range in size from the Greater Glider, which is about the size of a brushtail or ringtail possum, down through intermediate Squirrel Glider and Sugar Glider to the mouse-sized Feathertail or Pigmy Glider.

The Feathertail closely resembles the pigmy possums, of which it could be described as a flying version, and from which it differs most obviously in having the typical gliding membranes and the feathery-edged tail. Like them, the Feathertail at night seeks the nectar of flowering trees, and snatches up any insects it may discover.

In this action sequence, while one Feathertail feeds at the flowers of a north Queensland eucalypt, a second glider, dropping from a higher branch, comes in to land. Clearly visible are the sideways extensions of body skin which stretch between front and hind limbs to give a wide parachute surface, and the feathery-fringed tail that gives control during flight. Australia has only this one species of mouse-sized glider, *Acrobates pygmaeus,* which inhabits eucalypt forests of eastern Australia, from north-eastern Queensland to South Australia.

Left: Australia has 24 species of the small, long-tailed birds known as wrens. These are subdivided into 3 main groups: the fairy wrens, the emu-wrens, and the grass-wrens. Of all these, it is one of the fairy wren group that is best known to the Australian public. This, the superb Blue Wren *(Malurus cyaneus)* in distribution exactly covers Australia's region of greatest human population, the south-eastern corner from Brisbane through Sydney and Melbourne to Adelaide, and throughout Tasmania. Here the birds inhabit the undergrowth of open forests and woodlands. Favourable conditions consist of dense ground cover of tangled bushes, bracken or tall grass beneath trees of woodlands or open forest.

Right: A tall slender shrub with showy pink flowers, Match Heads *(Conesperma ericinum)* is a common wildflower of the eucalypt forests of the granite country of the ranges of south-eastern Queensland, New South Wales, and Victoria. It flowers between September and December. The common name is derived from the match-head shape of the closed flower buds.

Left: Wandoo Trees *(Eucalyptus wandoo)* in the Dryandra State Forest are of a species of tree which may grow either as open forest, or as woodland. Those closer to the coast or in wetter valleys tend to be larger, more closely spaced, and conform to a description of dry eucalypt forest. Areas on drier hilltops, or further inland, have smaller, more widely spaced trees, making a typical woodland habitat. The transition between forest and woodland can be without clear boundary. Open dry eucalypt forest has a variety of wildlife, including the interesting small marsupials, the Numbat and the Woilie, a rat-kangaroo.

Right: Firetail finches inhabit localities of dense coastal vegetation of both eastern and south-western Australia. One species, restricting itself to the most arid of northern spinifex country, is the exception. There are five species of the firetail group, all with a brilliant red on the rump and upper tail-coverts. Those inhabiting the eastern and south-eastern forests are the Red-browed Firetail, the Diamond Firetail, and the Beautiful Firetail. The south-western Australia species is the Red-eared Firetail *(Emblema oculata),* shown in this photograph. It is a shy secretive species, of very restricted distribution, inhabiting dense vegetation of dry sclerophyll forests, and thickets of coastal heathlands. For such a small bird, the nest is a very bulky structure, shaped like, and almost as large as, a football lying on its side, but with a long entrance spout. Despite its bulk, the nest is rarely conspicuous, being placed in a dense clump of foliage.

Right: The grass-tree or blackboy is a characteristic element of the Australian bush, particularly the tall, many-forked old specimens, which reach 4 or 5 m in height. The flowers are massed together on a tall white or pale yellow spike held high above. Although the blackboy is unharmed by the most intense of fires, and afterwards is one of the first plants in the bush to send out new foliage, the charred trunk remains black for many years. The leaves are long, slender, very rigid and usually brittle. The dead leaf mass is a favoured nesting place for birds. Some fifteen species of this genus, *Xanthorrhoea,* are found in most States except the Northern Territory.

Above and left: The Square-tailed Kite is found throughout Australia except for the heavily forested eastern and south-eastern coasts and ranges. But in most parts it is a rather rare bird. Kites are medium-large birds of prey which do not capture their prey by speed or power of attack as do eagles, falcons and hawks. Rather they fly more slowly, often soaring and gliding, floating through the treetops or over the plains, to drop on to small creatures on the ground, or on foliage. The Square-tailed Kite (*Lophoictinia isura*) hunts in this manner, floating quite slowly on long broad wings just above the treetops, snatching insects and small lizards from leaves or branches. In this way they also find many nests of small birds. The Square-tailed Kite is a beautifully plumaged species when seen at close range, and is also an incredibly placid and gentle bird at its nest. With delicate touch of cruel-looking claws and hooked bill, the Kite tears up the prey and then gently offers tiny pieces at the tip of its bill to the fluffy white chick.

Right: Sugar Gliders are tough, adaptable, widespread and probably the most abundant of Australia's gliding marsupials. They are found in woodlands and forests of eastern Australia, and across northern Australia as far west as the Kimberley region, in climates ranging from sub-zero alpine to tropical heat. The success of this species may partly derive from its tolerance of habitats ranging from open savannah woodlands to the tall close-packed eucalypts of south-eastern forests, and climates from tropical heat to sub-zero alpine. Sugar Gliders seem to accept almost anything edible that the bush has to offer. Their liking for sweet substances, such as the gum that exudes from the bark of some eucalypts, and for nectar, has given them their name. But insects and spiders are sought even more eagerly, and occasionally much larger prey. One of these gliders in the Kimberleys, was eating a small dove when lit up by the beam of a spotlight. The diet of captive gliders suggests that a wide variety of native fruits would be eaten when available. The Sugar Glider *(Petaurus breviceps)* is a gregarious species.

Right: The Rainbow Lorikeet *(Trichoglossus haematodus)* is the best known of Australian lorikeets, for it inhabits the forests of the eastern coast and ranges from southern New South Wales to Cooktown in northern Queensland. It has been brought to public attention at Currumbin on the southern Queensland coast, where many hundreds of these birds come each day to feed upon a honey mixture, perching upon the tourists in their eagerness to get at food. This pair was photographed in the wild, resting upon the hollow limb which was their nest, beside the Gilbert River, north Queensland. Rainbow Lorikeets, feeding in the tops of flowering trees, are conspicuous for their noisy screeching. A flock of these birds, their plumage brilliant in the sunlight, dashing through the treetops, always makes a spectacular sight. They are nomadic, the flocks wandering extensively in search of flowering trees, to feed on nectar, pollen, insects and fruits.

Left: Ringing whip-crack calls, repeated constantly, make the Golden Whistler a bird difficult to overlook in Australia's forests in the spring months. Once seen, its bold gold, black and white colours make it easily recognized. In contrast to the male, the female is plumaged in light greyish tones; males take several years to develop their colourful plumage, and for a time resemble the females. Quite closely related to the flycatcher family, Whistlers are larger, more solidly built and slower moving. They rarely catch insects in flight, but find them on foliage and bark of trees. While the Golden Whistler is the most colourful species, its song does not compare with that of the Rufous Whistler. The Golden Whistler *(Pachycephala pectoralis)* inhabits forests of eastern, south-eastern and south-western Australia. Its wide distribution gives rise to slight variations of plumage, so that, within Australia, some 14 slightly differing forms have been recognized. The male Golden Whistler does much of the incubation of the eggs and feeding of the young.

Right: The rather fearsome-looking Bearded Dragon rarely tries to escape by running, but relies upon camouflage colours to avoid being seen. Being quite a large reptile, up to 60 cm in length and stoutly built, it takes some time to warm up and become active on a cold morning, and will seek a warm surface, sometimes a road. The Bearded Dragon is actually a group of seven very similar species, not a single species. Between them, they cover most of the continent. The best known of these is the eastern coastal species *Amphibolurus barbatus.* In dry regions of Queensland and New South Wales its place is taken over by a superficially almost identical species, *Amphibolurus vitticeps,* and other closely similar species extend further westward. The common names Bearded Dragon or Jew Lizard apply to most species.

Left: A bold contrast in red and black makes this spider attractive yet signals a warning. But despite its colours, it is harmless. Commonly found under rocks and logs in the drier forests and woodlands, the Red and Black Spider *(Nicodamus bicolor)* in brilliance of colour by far surpasses its deadly relative, the Red Back Spider. The female of this species grows to a body length of about 14 mm, while the male has a relatively smaller body but longer legs. The webs of this species are rather untidy structures usually near the ground, beside or partially under rocks or logs.

Left: Probably the most appealing of the small marsupials are the pigmy possums, with their bulging black eyes, delicate big floppy ears, feet that are like tiny human hands, long clinging tail and fine soft fur. Sometimes when found, perhaps in a hollow tree or old bird's nest, they will be in a semi-hibernating condition, tightly rolled into a ball shape, big soft ears folded down over sleepy eyes, tail tightly curled. But when fully awakened, hunting for insects and feeding on nectar of flowering trees, they move quickly through the foliage, aided by the grip of their prehensile tails, often making leaps from twig to twig. Australia has four pigmy possum species. The Eastern Pigmy Possum inhabits forests and woodlands of south-eastern Australia and Tasmania, while this Western Pigmy Possum *(Cercartetus concinnus)* occurs in western New South Wales, the south-east of South Australia, and the south-western forests of Western Australia. The Little Pigmy Possum is found in Tasmania, while the Long-tailed Pigmy Possum is confined to north-eastern Queensland.

Right: Two species of Australian honeyeaters have beaks which, for such small birds, are very long and slender, an appropriate basis for the name 'spinebill'. With these birds the honeyeater bill reaches its greatest development, perfectly suited to probing into deep narrow tubular flowers from which other birds would have difficulty in obtaining nectar. Both the Australian spinebill species are restless, active birds, with erratic flight patterns; often insects are pursued and caught in the air in aerobatic twisting and turning. The Eastern Spinebill inhabits the coastal heaths and forests from Cooktown to Adelaide, while the Western Spinebill *(Acanthorhynchus superciliosus)* shown here, is confined to the south-west corner of the continent. Cross-pollination occurs among the flowers at which this bird feeds with its long bill.

WET EUCALYPT FORESTS

The eucalypt forests of the high rainfall regions of south-eastern and south-western Australia are among the most awe-inspiring of living wonders of Australia. Trees soar upwards to tremendous heights. Their straight, smooth trunks, white-tinted with grey or ochre tones, rise like columns from the undergrowth, and soar thirty metres or more to their first branches. The graceful lines of their limbs and trunks continue upward still higher, branching again and again until merging with the canopy of leaves, so far above that they seem to belong with sky and clouds rather than with the earth.

At the feet of the forest giants is a cool, damp, shaded world. Here the sunlight is broken by the veil of foliage far above, green-filtered, yet not so dark or gloomy as to prevent the growth of a luxuriant understorey of smaller trees, shrubs, treeferns, creepers and climbing plants.

This type of forest, here called for convenience wet eucalypt forest, is more precisely known as wet sclerophyll forest. The term 'sclerophyll' refers to the harder, stiffer leaves of the eucalypts compared with soft-leaved rainforest trees.

In the visual impact of sheer overwhelming mass of vegetation, the wet sclerophyll forests can equal the rainforests, yet be totally different. Where mature rainforests carry the great mass of their foliage in their high levels, and seem almost empty below, these eucalypt forests are heavily vegetated in their lower strata, more open where the giants lift clear of the lesser trees.

The wet sclerophyll forests have an understorey of small trees, shrubs and herbs. In some parts of Australia, many of the understorey plants are rainforest species. This type of forest develops in localities of higher rainfall and better soils.

Unlike the tremendous diversity of intermixed tree species encountered in tropical and sub-tropical rainforests, the wet sclerophyll forests tend to foster a single dominant species in any one locality, for example Mountain Ash in south-eastern Australia, the Karri in south-western Australia and the Rose Gum in the Brisbane area. The trees of these forests are usually tall, often very tall, and at least half the total height is made up of the massive bole section before the branched and foliage-bearing portion of the tree is reached.

Wet sclerophyll forest is found in some of the heaviest rainfall areas around the coasts of the southern half of Australia, from the Central Queensland coast to Victoria to Tasmania, and in the extreme south-western corner of Western Australia. The character of the forests changes, with different trees and undergrowth species from one region to another. A wet sclerophyll forest of the east coast may share no species of tree or other plant with a wet sclerophyll forest of south-western Australia. Yet the overall appearance and character of the two forests can be so similar that they will be recognized as being of the same class of habitat. This is true, although each may share plant species with dry sclerophyll or rainforest, and be on opposite sides of the continent.

Some of the most spectacular of wet sclerophyll forests are those of the mountainous south-east of Australia. Such forests are a striking feature of the Victorian natural environment, with the forests of the south-eastern mountain chain extending westwards to the suburbs of Melbourne.

In this region, high year-round rainfall and rich volcanic soil have permitted the growth of some magnificent eucalypt forests. Well known is Sherbrook Forest Park, where occur stands of Mountain Ash, Messmate and Mountain Grey Gum, with an understorey of Sassafras, Musk Daisybush and Blackwood. In damp situations, as along streams, are Soft Tree-ferns, and many mosses, lichens and smaller ferns. Further east, on the slopes of the Australian Alps, are greater tracts of such forests. In the Cumberland Valley are some of the tallest of Mountain Ash to be found on the Australian mainland.

Wet sclerophyll forest is a dominant feature of the Otway Ranges of south-coastal Victoria. A combination of heavy rainfall and rich soil has produced a dense cover of tall trees. The tallest trees are eucalypts, the Mountain Ash, Mountain Grey Gum, Southern Blue Gum and Alpine Ash. With the eucalypts grow rainforest species, including the Antarctic Beech. The dense canopy of foliage and the dim cool environment at the lower levels have encouraged the growth of many epiphytes and lichens, while treeferns are abundant. These dense strata of vegetation in some places allow so little light to reach the forest floor that, like the rainforest floor, the ground is almost bare.

Wet sclerophyll forest is a major natural habitat of Australia's east coast, and can most easily be seen in the many national parks. Morton National Park, near Robertson, has

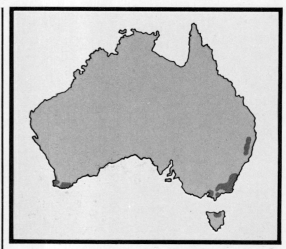

such forest, as well as rainforest, along the moist lower slopes of its escarpment. Deep valleys of the Blue Mountains have forests of huge Blue Gums. On the mountain slopes of Kosciusko National Park, below 1300 metres altitude, grow tall Mountain Ash and Stringy Bark trees.

In northern New South Wales, wet eucalypt forests are a feature of Barrington Tops and Gloucester Tops National Parks. Further north, wet sclerophyll forest grows on moist basaltic soils of the eastern slopes of the New England Tableland, and can be seen in the National Parks of the region, New England National Park, Guy Fawkes National Park and Gibraltar Range National Park.

In south-eastern Queensland, usually along the ranges and some parts of the coastal lowlands, wet sclerophyll forests have a canopy of very tall trees, such as the Rose Gum, with an understorey of smaller trees and shrubs, many of which are rainforest species in the shelter of the big gums.

The Karri forests of the south-western corner of the continent can be seen in Nornalup National Park, Warren National Park and various other reserves within the rather restricted area in which this type of forest reaches its magnificent climax.

Opposite page: Trees of coastal wet eucalypt forest rise from dense undergrowth characteristic of this habitat. Wet eucalypt forest, more accurately described as wet sclerophyll forest, is most widespread in mountainous south-eastern Australia and Tasmania, with a small area in the south-west of the continent.

Right: The Common Ringtail *(Pseudocheirus peregrinus)* is an extremely widely distributed denizen of Australian forests. Its distribution ranges from north-eastern Queensland right around the eastern forested coastal belt of New South Wales and Victoria to forested parts of South Australia, Western Australia and Tasmania. In common with other very widely distributed animals, the most distant and isolated populations have tended to evolve slight differences. While not sufficient to make them separate species, these have distinct local common names, and are listed as sub-species. Thus there is a North Queensland Ringtail, and in south-western Australia, isolated by the treeless Nullarbor, there is the dark-furred Western Ringtail, shown here. The characteristic feature of all ringtail possums is their long prehensile tail, often carried rolled into a tight ring shape when not being used as a 'fifth hand' for climbing.

Left: From the peeling bark that clings around its base, the massive trunk of the forest giant soars as a straight perfectly cylindrical column into the sky. It is awe-inspiring to stand beneath and look vertically upwards, when the huge tree seems to be toppling as clouds move overhead. Far above, foliage is buffeted by the wind, yet below, it is calm. Some of Australia's tallest eucalypts grow in opposite corners of the continent, the Mountain Ash in south-eastern Australia and the Karri in the south-west. In appearance the trees are similar, both having very tall trunks, not exceptional girth, and rather small crowns.

Right: Beneath towering eucalypts of the Tasmanian wet sclerophyll forest, tall tree-ferns form a dense understorey. In contrast to the rainforests, where a closed canopy of foliage shuts out so much light that there is almost no understorey, the eucalypt forest has a high but broken canopy. Far below, the spreading, interlacing fronds of the treeferns make a second, lower canopy in this forest on Mount Field National Park, south-western Tasmania. Below there is a dimly lit, wet environment where many mosses and shield ferns cover the ground and the fibrous trunks of the treeferns. A similar treefern understorey can also be found beneath wet sclerophyll forests of mainland Australia, especially in Victoria, where Ferntree Gully in the Dandenongs, and Tarra Valley in the Strzelecki Ranges of south Gippsland, are easily accessible examples.

Above: Potoroos are very small members of the Kangaroo family. They resemble bandicoots in appearance and in their habit of digging and scratching about in the leaf-litter and soil beneath dense undergrowth. The Southern Potoroo *(Potorous tridactylus)* has a head-and-body length of only 35 cm, and is uncommon except in Tasmania; this animal has also been listed as *Potorous apicalis.* Small members of the kangaroo family have suffered heavily from predation by foxes, and on the mainland the Potoroo is confined to small areas of suitable habitat along coastal parts of eastern Queensland and New South Wales. This defenceless marsupial is absolutely dependent upon the preservation of the natural vegetation for its survival. The usual habitat is low-lying localities, where concealment from predators is afforded by very dense undergrowth and herbage. Potoroos do not venture out to feed in open areas, but keep beneath dense

cover, digging for roots and tubers of plants at night, and hiding by day in a nest built in the thickest vegetation.

In common with many species of marsupials, and with Australian fauna and flora in general, the Potoroo has been the subject of considerable name-changing. Some references list this animal as *Potorous tridactylus,* others as *P. apicalis.* The name to be used depends upon whether the Tasmanian potoroos and those of the islands of Bass Strait, southern Victoria and South Australia, all the southern regions, are to be regarded as a full species separate from the potoroo of east-coastal New South Wales and Queensland. If they are a separate species, then the potoroo shown in the photograph is *Potorous apicalis,* being a southern animal.

On the other hand, if the southern potoroos are merely a sub-species of the east-coastal species, then they, like the east-coastal special, are *Potorous tridactylus,* sub-species *apicalis.* To

further complicate the matter, a potoroo which inhabited the south-west corner of Western Australia but which now is probably extinct, Gilberts Potoroo *(Potorous gilberti),* has been listed in some reference works as a distinct separate species. But more recent studies include this potoroo within the species *tridactylus,* that is *Potorous tridactylus gilberti.* Currently there is considered to be a single species, *tridactylus* with several sub-species. There is also another south-western potoroo, the Broad-faced Potoroo, *Potorous platyops,* which has been left as a full separate species. This appears almost certainly to be extinct.

A wide choice of common names includes that for the southern animal, known as the Southern Potoroo, or simply as Potoroo. The east-coastal animal is referred to as Long-nosed Rat-kangaroo or as Potoroo, while in Western Australia there are Gilberts Potoroo and the Broad-faced Potoroo.

Left: Darting into its nest, a tunnel drilled into a creek bank, this male Spotted Pardalote *(Pardalotus punctatus)* shows the patterns of spots on its wings and head responsible for this name. Bright colours to throat and rump make the tiny bird one of the jewels of the forests. Although the Spotted Pardalote is a bird of the treetops for most of the year, in the nesting season it comes down to the ground. In an earth bank, or in soil among the roots of a fallen tree, it drills a tunnel only about 25 mm across but 400 to 600 mm deep. Within the chamber at the end of the tunnel the industrious little birds construct a globular nest with soft dry materials, largely strips of bark. Here both male and female share the incubation of the eggs and the feeding of the young. Spotted Pardalotes are fast-flying, and approach the tunnel entrance at considerable speed, folding their wings as they dive into the opéning, so that they appear to fly straight in. These photographs show a sequence as the male Pardalote dives towards the entrance; they freeze fast action that, to the eye, is but a momentary blur of movement too rapid to allow study of detail. Visible are the workings of the flight feathers, which change between upstroke and downstroke, and the braking action to check the speed.

In the treetops, Spotted Pardalotes have specialized in the taking of insects from leaves and flowers, and often arrive at the nest with a beakful of tiny insects, yellow with pollen. These birds inhabit the forests of eastern, south-eastern, and south-western Australia, and Tasmania. Australia has eight species of pardalotes, some confined to far northern regions.

Previous page: The eastern escarpment of the New England Tableland is one of the most rugged regions of north-eastern New South Wales. From a plateau rim as high as 1600 m above sea level, the land plunges in steep gorges to the coastal plains. These slopes partly carry rainforest and, elsewhere, extensive tracts of wet sclerophyll forests. This panorama is to the south-east, from a high lookout beside the Gwydir Highway between Grafton and Glen Innes. In the mid-distance are the deep gorges of the Mann and Boyd Rivers. In the far distance are the highest parts of the escarpment in Guy Fawkes National Park and even further away, New England National Park.

Left: Found only in the eucalypt forests of the extreme south-west corner of Western Australia, the Red-winged Wren *(Malurus elegans)* keeps to the dense undergrowth of river valleys. It has a preference for moist localities, which has given it an alternative name of Marsh Wren. The nest of this species is rather different from most other wrens, being built of bulkier materials than the usual grass. Dead gum leaves form a considerable part of the structure, but at the expense of strength — if handled, the nest readily begins to disintegrate. A favourable location for the nest is close to the ground, where the 'skirt' of dead leaves of a low grass-tree touch the ground. Although the breast of this wren is actually a very dark blue, under most natural lighting conditions of the forest it appears black. The call is sufficiently distinctive to separate it in the field.

Above: The wet sclerophyll forests of Tasmania include some of Australia's tallest trees. This giant is in the Mount Field National Park. The tallest of Tasmanian eucalypts are the Mountain Ash *(Eucalyptus regnans)*, the Alpine Ash *(E. delegatensis)*, the Tasmanian Blue Gum *(E. globulus)* and Manna Gum *(E. viminalis)*. These giants grow on the damp fertile soils as in the valleys of the Styx, Arve, Picton and Florentine Rivers. The Mountain Ash is the world's tallest hardwood tree.

Left: Orchids adorn many of the mossy boulders of the coastal ranges of eastern Australia. The Pink Rock Orchid *(Dendrobium kingiania)* is a leafy spreading plant which forms extensive clumps across mossy boulders. The many short racemes of flowers are usually pink, but vary from white to deep pink. A second pink-flowered rock orchid of north-eastern New South Wales and southern Queensland is the Ravine Orchid *(Sarcochilus fitzgeraldii)*.

Left: Flying in to its nest in a hollow tree trunk, a Crimson Rosella *(Platycercus elegans)* displays colourful patterns of plumage which can only be seen by action-stopping high speed photography. The ability to fly is probably the most distinctive characteristic of birds, and one which determines almost every detail of their form, but especially the plumage. To be able to see the bird in flight, every feather functioning to achieve speed and control through the air, is to be able to appreciate the aesthetics of the bird as a creature of functional beauty, evolved for flight. The Crimson Rosella inhabits forests of the coastal ranges, from Brisbane to Adelaide, and also in north-eastern Queensland.

Left: The Red-necked Wallaby inhabits coastal scrubs and brush country from eastern Queensland through eastern New South Wales and southern Victoria to south-eastern South Australia, the Bass Strait islands, and Tasmania. Over this wide range it is known by many names, including Brush Wallaby, Brush Kangaroo, Scrub Wallaby, Roany, Bennetts Wallaby and, in Tasmania, simply as Kangaroo. The name Red-necked Wallaby refers to the reddish tone of the back of the neck and the shoulders, as does its scientific name, *Macropus rufogriseus*. It tends to keep to forest undergrowth where it browses on foliage, a habit which is reflected in many of the regional names, such as Scrub Wallaby and Brush Kangaroo.

Right: From forested heights of the Gibraltar Range, in north-eastern New South Wales, are extensive views over the deep river gorges of the eastern escarpment of the New England Tableland. Gibraltar Range projects as an eastwards spur of the Great Dividing Range, midway between Grafton and Glen Innes on the Gwydir Highway. The huge scale of these ranges can be deceptive, for the ranges which seem to be just across the valley would be a full day's bushwalking away, down precipitous slopes, through dense rainforests. The wet sclerophyll forests along these wet eastern slopes have as dominant trees the Tallowwood *(Eucalyptus microcorys)*, Sydney Blue Gum *(E. saligna)*, Rose Gum *(E. grandis)*, and Deane's Gum *(E. deanei)*.

Right: Mature Karri forest is among the natural wonders of Australia, the straight smooth trunks, white or buff-coloured, rising like columns from undergrowth. Passing through the crowns of the lower storey trees of banksia and peppermint, they rise 30 m or more to their first limbs. At the feet of the Karris' massive columns is a cool, damp and shaded world. The undergrowth contains many flowering shrubs and small trees, the Karri Hazel with creamy-white flowers, the Karri Wattle of pale gold, the Holly Flame Pea with flowers of flame red, the Tree Hovea of deep blue, and the Cutleaf Hibbertia with rich yellow flowers. In spring the undergrowth is transformed with creepers, the white Clematis, the purple of Sarsaparilla, and the flame red of the Coral vine. When these forests are in flower in summer, they are visited by Purple-crowned Lorikeets, tiny nectar-eating parrots. Predominantly green, and not much larger than a leaf, these birds are difficult to detect high in the Karris, where they would pass unnoticed but for their incessant noise. At other times, White-tailed Black Cockatoos are raucously present in the treetops.

Left: Australia has four species of yellow-breasted robins, and of these, the Eastern Yellow Robin (*Eopsaltria australis*) is the most brightly coloured, with yellow covering almost the entire undersurface of the body. In the forests the Eastern Yellow Robin sits quietly on a perch, or often clings motionless to the side of a treetrunk, where it may go unseen until it drops to the ground to capture an insect or other small creature. This species favours forests and woodlands where there is scrubby undergrowth, mainly in coastal districts from north-eastern Queensland to the south-eastern corner of South Australia.

Right: Many of Australia's wildflowers have evolved to their present forms to achieve greater success in pollination. It is of advantage to the plant that its pollen is transferred to flowers of the same species efficiently, not scattered uselessly among various wildflowers. Many Australian wildflowers have adapted to use birds rather than insects as their pollinators. The large tubular flowers of the Christmas Bell (*Blandfordia nobilis*) of New South Wales and southern Queensland is shaped so that the bird must thrust its head deep into the flower tube, so pollen is daubed on its head. The Yellow-faced Honeyeater (*Lichenostomus chrysops*) occurs in coastal forested regions of eastern and south-eastern Australia.

Right: The Crested Hawk is unusual among Australian birds of prey not only for its appearance, but also for its method of hunting. Its long broad wings give a rather slow buoyant flight, allowing it to float slowly through the treetops, where it snatches insects from the foliage. Here the Crested Hawk holds a leafy twig which it has brought in to add to the nest. A neat, pointed little crest at the back of its head completes a neat plumage of delicate grey tones, buff barred underparts, accentuated by bright yellow eyes. This rather uncommon hawk, scientifically named *Aviceda subcristata,* occurs along the forested eastern coast from Sydney to Cape York, and in tropical woodlands of the Northern Territory and Kimberleys.

Following page: This cloud-capped mountain top is far higher than any other range in Australia. From a line of peaks, including Mt. Kosciusko, Mt. Townsend, Mt. Twynham and Mt. Ramshead, the range on its north-western side drops precipitously to the Geehi Gorge, some 1500 m below. On the south-east slopes are forests of great Mountain Ash, Candlebark and Stringybark trees, which at higher altitudes give way to stunted Snow Gums and alpine heathlands.

Australian Vegetation Regions

The regions shown on the map are approximate, in order to show in a simplified manner, the locations of the habitats described in the text. Few habitats have clearly defined boundaries, so that their recognition and extent is open to a wide range of interpretations. Many greatly differing vegetation maps of Australia have been published. Most agree on the location of the rainforests, for these have a distinct border, where closed rainforest meets open eucalypt forest as a seemingly solid green wall. Other vegetation communities merge imperceptibly, and extensive transitional regions may be of intermixed or intermediate characteristics. Often there is a mosaic, where different types of vegetation dominate in patches too small to show on a map of this scale. Australia has no true deserts, but rather the mulga, spinifex and other arid vegetation is spread almost throughout the interior. However, a few regions well known by the term 'desert', are on average the most arid parts.

These include the Simpson Desert, the Tanami, Gibson, Great Sandy, and Victorian Deserts. Wetlands, comprising individual lakes or swamps, are too small to show individually upon a map of this scale. Australian wetlands occur in regions of heaviest rainfall, most commonly on coastal plains or river floodplains. Their major areas include tropical northern coastal river floodplains, the eastern and south-eastern coastal rivers and coastal plains, the south-west corner of Western Australia, and the Murray-Darling river system.

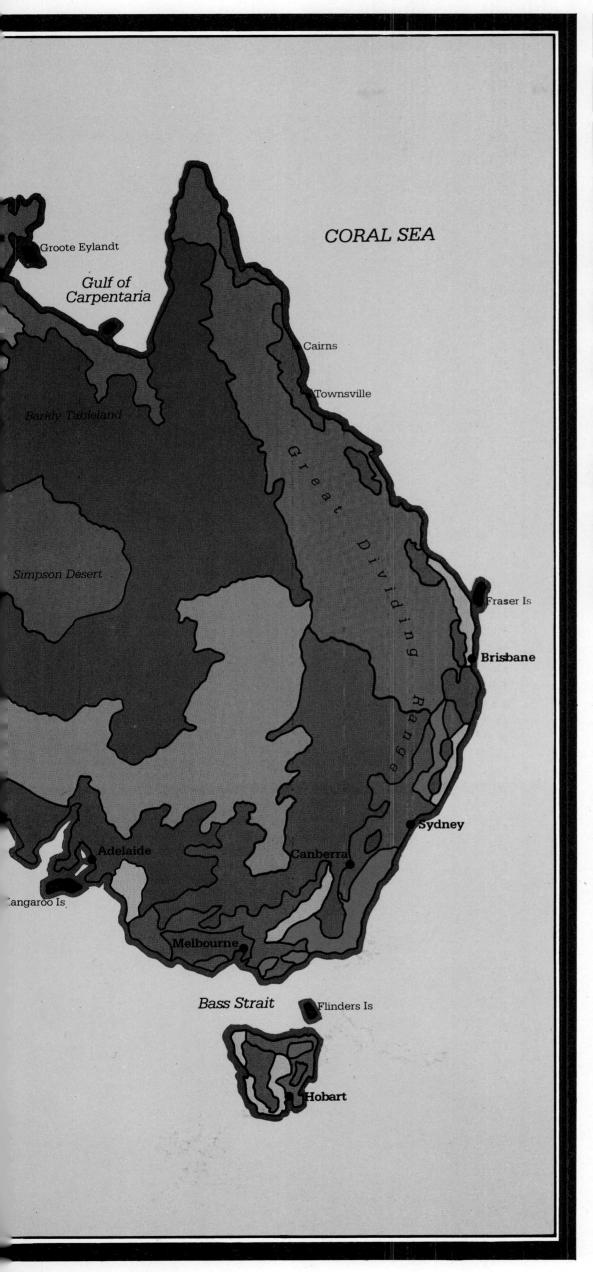

Heathlands and Sandplains

Spinifex and Other Arid Grasslands

Tropical and Temperate Rainforests

Mulga and Other Acacia Scrublands

Tropical Forests and Woodlands

Deserts and Arid Steppe-lands

Temperate and Alpine Woodlands

Coasts and Island Sanctuaries

Mallee and Arid Woodlands

Dry Eucalypt Forests

Wet Eucalypt Forests

CORAL SEA

Groote Eylandt

Gulf of Carpentaria

Barkly Tableland

Cairns

Townsville

Great Dividing Range

Simpson Desert

Fraser Is

Brisbane

Sydney

Adelaide

Canberra

Kangaroo Is

Melbourne

Bass Strait

Flinders Is

Hobart

INDEX

Page numbers in italic indicate photographs.

Published by Lansdowne Press Sydney

176 South Creek Road, Dee Why West,
NSW, Australia 2099
First published 1980
© Copyright: Michael Morcombe 1980
Produced in Australia by the Publisher
Typeset in Australia by Smith & Miles
Set in Serifa
Printed in Australia by Griffin Press Limited

National Library of Australia Cataloguing-in-Publication Data

Morcombe, Michael K.
  Australia the wild continent.

  Index
  ISBN 0 7018 1427 6

  1. Natural history — Australia.
  I. Title.

574.994

Acknowledgements

The author wishes to thank all those
who have given assistance over many
years, and extends thanks to the
following in particular:

  Frank Bailey, Lindsay Barnett,
Dr Andrew Burbridge, John Davey,
Ian Edgar, Ray Garstone, Alex George,
Doug Gilmore, John Hanrahan, the late
Jim Hargreaves, Max Howard, Bernie
Hyland, David James, Ron Johnstone,
Dave Kabay, Jeff Keen, Nicolas Kolichis,
Jeffrey Lewis, Malcolm Lewis, Dave
Lindner, Dr Neville Marchant, Maurie
Marshall, Roy Mercer, Barry Muir,
Owen Nichols, John Nixon, Roly Paine,
Greg Perry, Mike Pople, John Purdey,
Dr W. D. L. Ride, Peter Slater, Ray
Smith, Roy Stirling, Brian Wake, Norm
Wamsley, Betty Wellington, Bert Wells,
Alec Wood, Laurie Smith,
Phil (Jim Jim Falls).

  Department of Fisheries and
Fauna, Perth and Geraldton; West
Australian Agricultural Protection
Board; Tom Spence and Roy Fairfax,
Zoological Gardens Board.

  A Range Rover is currently used
for outback travelling.

For most of the photographs in *Australia
The Wild Continent,* a medium format
Mamiya RB67 camera, with lenses from
65 mm wideangle to 500 mm telephoto
has been used. In the case of birds in
flight, and for nocturnal animals, a high-
speed Multiblitz 3b has been used,
giving action-stopping speed of about
1/6000 of a second. Various colour films
have been used, initially Ektachrome E2,
later Agfachrome, and in recent years,
Ektachrome E6.

Designed by **Warren Penney**
Edited by **Peita Royle**